EAT MEDITERRANEAN

By the same author

Fresh Bread in the Morning From Your Bread Machine
Ice 'n' Easy
The Blender Book
Steaming!
Microwave Cooking Times at a Glance
The Combination Microwave Cook

Uniform with this book

EAT
MEDITERRANEAN

Annette Yates

RIGHT WAY

Typeset in 10/11 pt Swiss 721 by Letterpart Ltd., Reigate, Surrey.

Printed and bound in Great Britain by Cox & Wyman Ltd., Reading, Berkshire.

The *Right Way* series is published by Elliot Right Way Books, Brighton Road, Lower Kingswood, Tadworth, Surrey, KT20 6TD, U.K. For information about our company and the other books we publish, visit our website at www.right-way.co.uk

CONTENTS

For all those friends and members of my family who continue to flatter me by requesting recipes for the dishes they have just eaten at my table.

INTRODUCTION

To cook and eat Mediterranean food is to take part in an exciting and ongoing culinary adventure. And I love it!

I'm talking about a cuisine that is bright, vibrant, healthy and joyous, with colours and flavours that are both evocative and intense.

The sheer sight of glistening olives and a string of garlic, the vivid colours of lemons and oranges, or a mound of ripe tomatoes, aubergines and courgettes, is enough to make me rush into the kitchen to make something Mediterranean. And while slicing and chopping, I'm probably recalling a sun-soaked holiday, a lazy lunch outside some taverna overlooking the blue-green sea, or a bustling market with its glorious displays of fresh foods, its colours, scents and noise.

The strength of Mediterranean cooking comes from using the freshest ingredients and preparing them with a satisfying simplicity. It is about relishing the freedom to add a handful of this or a handful of that; about swapping ingredients according to seasons and what's available in the market today.

It is about getting together with friends and family to share traditional dishes, recipes for which have been passed on to each new generation from mother to daughter. It is about dishes that appear on the tables of more than one country, the same dishes that with a subtle variation in ingredients become unique to a region or culture.

Eat Mediterranean is my contribution to *your* culinary adventure. The recipes are some of my favourites and all have their origins in the regions surrounding the Mediterranean Sea – from southern Europe, through the Middle East and round to North Africa. They couldn't be simpler to make and they are guaranteed to bring the flavours of the Mediterranean to your table at any time of the year.

Enjoy the adventure, have fun and good eating!

Annette Yates

RECIPE NOTES

All spoon measures are level unless otherwise stated.

For convenience, the ingredients are listed in the order in which they are used. Though they are given in imperial as well as metric, you will find the metric measurements easier to use.

Eggs are medium, unless otherwise stated. One or two recipes may contain raw or partly cooked eggs – please remember that it is advisable to avoid eating these if you are pregnant, elderly, very young or sick.

Some recipes are suitable for cooking in the microwave and the instructions given are for an 800W oven. If your microwave oven has a lower wattage, you will need to cook for a little longer. If it has a higher wattage, best results will be obtained by reducing the power level slightly and cooking for the time given in the recipe.

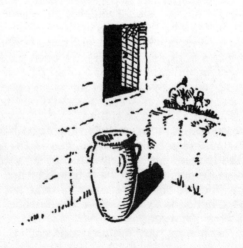

1

MEDITERRANEAN INGREDIENTS A-Z

Bulgur wheat
Bulgur wheat or burghul is made from wheat grains that have been steamed, dried and crushed into pieces. During cooking they swell and soften again ready for serving with meat, fish and vegetable dishes, or for adding to stuffings and salads, of which tabbouleh (page 49) is probably the best known.

Capers
A caper is the flower bud of a shrub that is native to the Mediterranean. Having been picked and left to dry, the capers are packed in vinegar or salt, which should be rinsed off before use. Capers have a strong, tangy flavour. They play a major role in making the olive paste Tapénade (page 26) and the green herb sauce Salsa Verde (page 67). They are also good in salads, added to mayonnaise and sauces, sprinkled on pizzas, and as a garnish with fish, vegetables or meat (particularly lamb).

Cheeses
Feta is a rindless white Greek cheese that is shaped into blocks and stored or packed in salty whey brine. The best is made from ewe's milk while the rest is made with goat's or cow's milk. Appreciate its tangy flavour by serving it simply with crusty bread or in a salad, Greek style with lettuce, tomatoes, olives and hard-boiled egg. Or add it to stuffings and savoury pastries such as Spinach and Cheese Pie (page 77) or crumble it into a vegetable risotto just before serving.
   Gruyère is originally from Switzerland but is now made in several other countries including France and Italy. It has a golden rind with a pale, creamy interior and its flavour is

distinctive, sweet and nutty. Gruyère melts well to make a delicious toasted sandwich. Grate it over soups and gratin dishes or add it to pasta and potato dishes.

Halloumi or halumi is a semi-hard cheese originally made in Cyprus with the milk of goats or ewes. Halloumi made in the UK usually contains cow's milk and tends to have a much harder texture. The best has a springy texture and slices well. Its flavour should be mild and slightly salty (like feta it is packed in whey brine). Unusually, halloumi retains its shape during heating – try frying or grilling slices quickly with olive oil until golden brown and serving them as an appetiser or with a salad of tomatoes and olives. Take care not to overcook it because it is likely to turn tough and leathery.

Manchego is a Spanish cheese that is now more readily available. It is a hard cheese made with ewe's milk and is particularly good served with bread or biscuits and quince preserve. Small cubes, plain or fried in olive oil, appear in Spanish tapas or appetisers.

Mascarpone is a rich Italian cheese made with cow's milk. It is soft, thick and creamy with a flavour that is quite delicate. Serve it in similar ways to thick cream – with fruit, cakes and puddings, and in desserts flavoured with coffee, chocolate or liqueur. Or stir it into pasta sauces and fillings for savoury tarts.

Mozzarella is a mild, fresh cheese from Italy. The best is made from the milk of water buffaloes though most of it is now made with cow's milk. It is stored or packed in mild brine. Drained, patted dry and sliced, it is good served with a salad of tomatoes, red onion slices and olives, all drizzled with a good-quality olive oil. Mozzarella features mainly in hot dishes – pizzas in particular, where it melts to a soft stretchy consistency. Like most cheeses, it tends to become stringy and tough when overcooked.

Parmesan is a matured, extra-hard, cheese with a granular texture, the best of which hails from Northern Italy and is called Parmigiano Reggiano (look for the name stamped on its shiny golden rind). It is made with unpasteurised cow's milk, has a strong flavour and keeps particularly well. Parmesan that is freshly grated is far superior to the ready-grated product. Use it on its own or with other cheeses when you want to add extra flavour. Sprinkle it on to vegetable soups and gratin dishes, or add shavings to salads and pasta dishes. Parmesan is an ingredient in pesto sauce (see page 65) and Aubergine Parmigiana (page 83).

Ricotta is a soft, white, Italian cheese that is made with the whey left over from other cheese production (the word ricotta means 'recooked'). It is extremely low in fat and has a delicate, fresh taste which makes it suitable for both savoury and sweet dishes. It is used in lasagne, cannelloni and ravioli; and in cheesecakes, fruit tarts, trifles and other puddings.

Chillies
Chillies, like sweet peppers, are members of the Capsicum family. Their colours range from yellow and green to red and black; some are long and thin while others are short and plump. Generally, the smaller the chilli the more pungent it is. The seeds and veins are the hottest parts and adding them to your dish together with the chilli flesh will make for an extra fiery result. The oils in chilli can cause severe burning on contact with the eyes and sensitive areas of skin, so take care when preparing them and wash your hands thoroughly afterwards or wear rubber gloves to handle them. When fresh chillies are not available, use the dried varieties – whole, flakes or ground. (See also Harissa, page 13.)

Coffee
Though freshly made strong coffee is drunk all over the Mediterranean, as an ingredient in cooking it is used mainly to flavour Italian desserts such as trifles and granitas.

Couscous
A principal ingredient in North African cuisines, couscous is made from ground semolina that has been moistened, shaped into tiny balls and rolled in flour. It is usually served as a grain alongside vegetable or meat stews (such as Spiced Lamb with Preserved Lemon on page 92). The word couscous can also refer to the complete dish – stew and grain together. The type available here in the UK is usually precooked and simply needs reconstituting briefly with hot water or stock. Combined with other ingredients, couscous is also good served hot or cold as a salad dish, as in Cinnamon-Scented Couscous with Onions, Fruit and Pine Nuts on page 53. It can be made into sweet dishes too.

Dried beans and peas
See pulses.

Fish

A huge variety of fish is available that, until recently, was mainly to be found around the Mediterranean, where each country seems to have its own version of fish soup (see page 38). As well as familiar species like cod, consider choosing sea bass, bream, John Dory, grouper, gurnard, hake, mackerel, monkfish, grey and red mullet, octopus, sardines, squid, swordfish and tuna. Shellfish is widely available too, including cockles, crab, lobster, mussels, prawns and scallops. Salt cod is popular in several Mediterranean countries, particularly in the Provence region of France where it is used to make brandade – a purée of well-soaked salt cod, garlic, olive oil and cream that is served with toast or fried bread. But perhaps the best-known Mediterranean fish is the anchovy, a tiny oily fish that simply bursts with flavour. Fresh ones are seldom to be found away from the Mediterranean. Instead, we can buy them filleted and packed in salt or oil, in jars and cans. Use just a few fillets to liven up a pizza topping (see Pissaladière on page 76) or a savoury tart filling. Anchovies are a principal ingredient in Anchoiade (page 70) and the green herb sauce called Salsa Verde (page 67). Only a little is needed to add an intense burst of flavour.

Fruit

It is almost impossible to think of the Mediterranean without picturing colourful markets with their mouth-watering displays of fruit. Think lemons, limes, oranges and grapefruit; apricots, peaches and nectarines; dates, figs and grapes; mangoes, melons and papaya; guavas, persimmons and pomegranates; apples, pears and plums; not to mention the seasonal soft fruits and a host of dried fruits. In summer, there is nothing nicer for dessert than a platter of ripe fresh fruit. Alternatively, why not serve a selection of dried fruits (apricots, dates and figs) together with some shelled nuts (almonds and walnuts are good)? Or make a simple but refreshing fruit salad with two or three types of fruit – such as melon, mango and grapes. Fruit that is unripe is ideal for poaching in syrup (try Pears in Rose Water on page 115) or for cooking in desserts like Peach and Almond Tart on page 110. Jellies need fruit that is ripe but firm, while really soft fruit is ideal for ice creams and sorbets. Fruit can figure in savoury dishes too – see Couscous with Apricots, Feta and Pine Nuts on page 79 and Cinnamon-Scented Couscous with Onions, Fruit and Pine Nuts on page 53.

Garlic

Garlic can transform an ordinary dish into something special. Rub a cut garlic clove over the inside of a salad bowl before adding the contents, or over toasted bread slices before adding your chosen topping. Heat a clove of garlic (finely chopped or crushed through a garlic press) in oil before adding the ingredients of a stew. Infuse some garlic slices gently in oil before lifting them out and frying fish or meat. Roasted whole in its skin, garlic cooks to a creamy softness and develops a lovely mild flavour – simply squeeze it out of its skin and spread it on bread or stir it into sauces and gravies. When choosing garlic, look for heads that are plump and firm.

Harissa

This fiery red paste, made with chilli, garlic and various spices, is common to North African dishes. Traditionally it might accompany couscous, served in a separate bowl and diluted with some of the liquid from the main dish, but it can also be added to soups, stews and other savoury dishes. Buy it in small quantities – it is usually fiery and a little goes a long way.

Herbs

Basil, known as the king of herbs, is best used raw or added to a hot dish at the last minute. Toss leaves into salads and pasta sauces and use it to make Italian Pesto (page 65). Dried basil has little flavour and is not worth using.

Bay leaves are used in marinades, soups, sauces and stews. Only one or two will be required in a dish especially when using the dried version, which tends to have a stronger flavour.

Chives add their fresh, mild, onion flavour to salads and yogurt dishes.

Coriander has flat tender leaves with a distinctive flavour that you either love or hate. Chop it into salads, rice dishes, sauces, soups and stews.

Dill with its feathery fronds goes well with eggs, fish and poultry. Like basil, it loses its flavour quickly on heating so add it to hot dishes just before serving.

Fennel has a mild aniseed flavour that complements fish in particular.

Mint is extremely popular in eastern and southern Mediterranean cooking, adding its freshness to drinks, vegetables, fish dishes, sauces, soups and stews. Mint is one of the few herbs that is worth buying dried.

Oregano or wild marjoram is an ancient herb that grows on the Greek hillsides and fills the air with its aroma. Sprinkle it on pizzas and breads, and add it to salads, soups, sauces, stews and anything containing tomatoes. Dried oregano is a good alternative to fresh.

Parsley, the flat leaf variety, is widely used around the Mediterranean in all sorts of dishes and in large quantities. Dried parsley, unfortunately, is no substitute for fresh.

Rosemary has a pungency that goes particularly well with meat, poultry and oily fish. Use small amounts to flavour soups, sauces and sweet dishes too. It grows all year round so there is no real need to use dried.

Sage is another pungent herb. Use it sparingly in stuffings and with meat and poultry. It goes well with eggs and cheese too.

Tarragon has a distinctive flavour that is especially good with chicken and fish. Add it to salads, sauces and marinades too.

Thyme grows wild in France and Greece, where it is used to flavour all sorts of dishes with vegetables, fish, poultry and meat. Dried thyme is a good substitute, even though fresh is available all year.

Honey
Honey is one of our oldest foods and is used all over the Mediterranean, mainly in sweet dishes. Choose one with a good flavour, such as Greek honey from bees that have visited wild thyme. Try it drizzled over juicy ripe fruit such as peaches and served with a generous helping of thick Greek yogurt. Honey is delicious added to Rice Pudding (page 121), Greek pastries such as Baklava (page 118) and cakes like Almond Cake with Lemon and Honey (page 122).

Lentils
See pulses.

Marsala
The sweet version of this famous fortified wine from Italy (Sicily actually) is used to flavour desserts such as Zabaglione (page 119).

Mastic

This is the dried aromatic resin that is gathered from the mastic tree. It is one of the ingredients of the sweetmeat Turkish delight. If you are lucky enough to obtain some mastic, crush just a little and add it to milk puddings.

Nuts

Nuts are used throughout the Mediterranean in vegetable and meat dishes, stuffings, salads and sauces, as well as a myriad of pastries and desserts. Almonds, hazelnuts, pistachios and walnuts can be used whole, chopped or ground. Pine nuts, the pale cream kernels extracted from the cone of the stone pine tree, are widely used in Middle Eastern dishes for their distinctive flavour and oily texture. Coconut is grated into desserts, cakes and biscuits. It's worth remembering that most nuts benefit from toasting to bring out their full flavour.

Oils

If a single ingredient were to evoke Mediterranean cooking it would surely be olive oil. Today we are fortunate to be offered a huge selection from several areas around the Mediterranean, including France, Greece, Italy and Spain, each with its own unique flavour. There is an olive oil to suit every occasion, every taste and every pocket. The finest (and therefore the most expensive) are from single estates, and then there are blends of oils and, finally, refined oils. For the best flavour choose those labelled 'cold pressed', 'extra virgin' and 'virgin' – these are produced from the first cold pressing of the ripe olives. They have an intensity that makes them perfect for serving just as they are, with bread for dipping, or for drizzling over salads, bruschetta, cooked vegetables, pasta, pizzas and soups. Blended and refined oils are the ones to use for cooking.

Olives

Olive trees grow all over the Mediterranean, producing fruit in a variety of shapes, sizes and colours. Once they are picked and cured, we can buy olives whole, pitted, marinated in flavoured oil or stuffed with the likes of anchovies, almonds, capers or pimento. Olives make a delicious appetiser before a meal or a tasty garnish for dishes like hummus (page 24). It takes hardly any time to whizz up a bowl of black or green olive paste (page 26). Or why not scatter them in salads, include them in bread dough and pizza toppings, or add them to tagines and stews (see Chicken with Olives and Preserved Lemon on page 102 and Slow-Cooked Beef in Red Wine on page 98)?

Orange flower water

This colourless liquid, produced by distilling the blossoms of bitter oranges, is used mainly to flavour sweet dishes. It is sprinkled over fruit, stirred into drinks and added to cakes, pastries and other puddings. In savoury dishes, it can be sprinkled over salads or stews. Orange flower water tends to be quite pungent, so add it carefully, a little at a time.

Pasta

Pasta, the versatile staple of Italy, is available fresh or dried in a range of shapes, sizes and flavours to suit all kinds of dishes and every occasion. It is made by mixing flour and water (and often egg) to form a dough, which is then kneaded and cut into shapes. Small shapes like shells, stars and strands are ideal for adding to soups. Long slender pasta, such as spaghetti and tagliatelle, are best served with a light dressing or sauce, while larger shapes such as bows, quills, twists and shells are designed to hold chunky sauces in their hollows, pockets and folds. Finally, there are flat sheets (lasagne) and large tubes (cannelloni) that are perfect for baking, plus a range of filled pastas like ravioli and tortellini.

Pastry

Filo pastry makes a regular appearance in Mediterranean cooking and is the one to use in Greek pastries such as Spinach and Cheese Pie (page 77) and Baklava (page 118). The Greek name for this pastry is phyllo (leaf), which aptly describes the paper-thin sheets of dough. Each layer is brushed with butter as the leaves are built up to make a crispy, flaky covering or parcel for savoury or sweet fillings. Filo pastry dries easily once its packet has been opened, so try to work quickly, keeping it covered in the meantime.

Polenta

This fine-ground cornmeal is popular in Northern Italy. Cooked to a thick purée and served with butter it makes a satisfying accompaniment to fish, meat, poultry and game dishes. When the purée is allowed to cool and firm up, it can be cut into pieces and fried or grilled with olive oil, or baked in the oven with a sauce such as tomato. Polenta goes particularly well with lamb, tomatoes and cheese such as Parmesan.

Pulses
Dried peas, beans and lentils are versatile ingredients that can be made into soups, stews and salads. Chickpeas are an important ingredient in traditional dishes such as Hummus (page 24) and Falafel (page 32). Whilst pulses keep well, they can become tough when stored too long, so it is a good idea to buy them in small quantities. Lentils can be cooked straight from the packet but beans and peas need to be soaked for several hours before cooking. Simply cover them with plenty of cold water and leave to stand for a few hours or overnight. Next day, drain them and cover with more cold water, then simmer gently until tender (cooking times vary according to the variety). Some beans, including red kidney and soy, should be boiled rapidly for 10 minutes to destroy toxins before simmering. Salt tends to toughen them so resist adding it until the beans or peas are tender. Canned varieties are ready cooked and can often make a convenient alternative to dried.

Rice
Rice features in many regions of the Mediterranean. Italian risottos are best made with short grain rice, such as arborio or carnaroli – the grains remain firm during cooking, absorbing plenty of flavour while swelling and clinging to each other to give a creamy consistency. For dishes where the rice grains need to be kept separate and dry, such as in salads (see Lentil and Rice Salad on page 54) and Middle Eastern pilaffs, long grain (patna) rice is the type to choose. The Spanish dish Paella (see page 86) is traditionally made with rice grown in the Valencia region, which becomes very tender during cooking without becoming creamy. (In the absence of 'paella' rice, risotto rice makes an acceptable alternative.) Milk puddings require starchy round or short grain rice that is capable of absorbing large amounts of liquid and cooks to a creamy mass (see Rice Pudding with Rose Water and Vanilla on page 121).

Rose water
This is the fragrant liquid produced by distilling rose petals and is the principal flavouring in the sweetmeat Turkish

delight. There are two types available – a mild diluted version that is inexpensive (generally sold in large clear bottles) and a highly concentrated version that is sold in small dark bottles and is more pricey. Whatever you use, add it gradually in small amounts and it will give a wonderful fragrance to fruit and sweet desserts; put in too much and you could end up with a dish that is overpoweringly perfumed.

Semolina

Semolina is coarsely ground durum wheat and is the main ingredient in good-quality dried pasta and in couscous. It is also used to make gnocchi (Italian dumplings), puddings, biscuits, cakes and confectionery.

Sesame seeds

These tiny seeds have a rich, sweet flavour that is enhanced by toasting. They can be used in bread, salads, dressings, savoury tarts, falafel (page 32), spice mixes such as Dukkah (page 27) and sweet dishes.

Spices

A wide range of spices is used all over the Mediterranean to season appetisers, main dishes and desserts. Most spices are available ready ground but, for the best flavour, buy them whole and grind them yourself, either with pestle and mortar or in a coffee grinder.

Allspice, not to be confused with mixed spice, is sold as whole berries or ground and supplies a flavour that is reminiscent of cloves, cinnamon and nutmeg. Use it in marinades, meat dishes and milk puddings and in desserts containing chocolate.

Cardamom is available as whole green pods or ground. Whole pods need to be cracked open to release the flavour of the seeds within. Cardamom enhances stews and dishes made with couscous, as well as desserts (it goes particularly well with oranges and melon), biscuits and cakes and Turkish coffee.

Cinnamon imparts its sweet fragrance to all sorts of meat dishes, sweet dishes and drinks. Buy it whole (like rolls of bark) or ground to a powder.

Coriander seeds have an orange-tasting sweetness and are often used together with cumin.

Cumin seeds have a pungent flavour. Teamed with coriander they provide a flavour that is characteristic of Mediterranean cooking. Add cumin to dips, marinades and sauces, and to fish, meat and vegetable dishes.

Nutmeg These large oval seeds are best freshly grated. Nutmeg goes particularly well with cheese, potatoes, spinach, squash and chicken, and adds its warm sweet flavour and aroma to sauces and custards.

Paprika is ground sweet red peppers and ranges from mild to hot. It can lose its flavour quickly during storage, so buy it in small quantities.

Pepper is probably the most important and fundamental of the spices. As well as adding its own flavour, it helps to bring out the flavour of other ingredients. Green peppercorns are the mildest, white pepper is hot, and black is the most pungent. Use whole peppercorns to flavour marinades, sauces and stews, otherwise freshly ground provides the best flavour.

Ras el hanout is a North African blend of spices that can include anise, cardamom, cinnamon, cloves, galangal, ginger, mace, nigella, nutmeg, peppercorns and turmeric. Sometimes it is perfumed with dried flowers such as damask rose and lavender. Add it to meat and game dishes, rice and couscous.

Saffron is the world's most costly spice and comprises the dried orange-red stamens of a purple-flowering crocus grown chiefly in Spain, Iran and Kashmir. Only a little is needed to impart its distinctive flavour and warm-yellow colour to all kinds of dishes – risotto, paella, soups, stews and tagines to name but some. Crush a few stamens or threads (with the back of a spoon or with pestle and mortar), soak them in a little hot liquid and allow the colour and flavour to seep out before adding it to your dish. Powdered saffron is a poor substitute.

Sumac is made from the berries of the sumac bush, which grows in the Middle East and parts of Italy. It has a sour flavour that is also fruity and in some cuisines it is used in place of lemon. Use the purple powder to season salad dressings and marinades and to sprinkle over fish dishes, grilled meats and salads just before serving.

Tamarind is the dark and sticky, sour-sweet pulp that surrounds the seeds in the pod of the tamarind tree. Its taste is slightly acidic. Choose whole pods and scrape out the pulp or buy tamarind as a paste or in blocks that require soaking in hot water before use.

Turmeric is often called 'poor man's saffron' though it tastes nothing like it. Turmeric looks like fresh root ginger but the flesh inside is a vibrant orange-yellow. Buy it whole for grating or ready ground. Just a small amount is needed to colour a dish and to add its warm spicy flavour.

Tahini
Tahini or tahina is a thick paste made with ground sesame seeds that is very popular in Middle Eastern cookery. Light tahini has had the seed husks removed and has a milder flavour than the dark version. Tahini is often stirred into dips and sauces, and savoury dishes that contain vegetables. It is an important ingredient in Hummus (page 24) to which it adds its rich sweetness.

Tomatoes
In Mediterranean countries fresh tomatoes of all shapes and sizes are to be found in abundance and at every stage of ripeness. In this country it's often not so easy – we seem to have plenty of firm, under-ripe tomatoes but obtaining ripe fruit bursting with that 'just-picked' and 'full of sunshine' flavour is often more difficult. If you are making a hot dish and fresh tomatoes are not up to scratch, use canned – they can be far superior, particularly in soups, sauces and stews – and add some chopped fresh tomato to liven up the dish at the last minute. Dried tomatoes are also useful for adding their chewy texture and intense flavour to sandwiches, soups, sauces, stuffings, stews and salads.

Vanilla
Vanilla pods are the dried, aromatic seed cases of an orchid. Split a pod lengthways, remove the seeds and use them to flavour ice creams and desserts (particularly those containing chocolate). Use the empty pod to infuse flavour into milk or cream when making custards or sweet sauces. Afterwards rinse and dry the pod and pop it in a jar of caster sugar to make vanilla sugar for sprinkling over fruit, biscuits and cakes. After vanilla pods, the next best thing is vanilla extract or essence, which contains the true flavour extracted from the pod – it is more costly than (but it is far superior to) any vanilla 'flavouring'. For a delicious vanilla dessert, try Panna Cotta on page 114.

Vegetables

Vegetables play a vital role in Mediterranean cooking and, thankfully, most of them are easily available. Choose from artichokes, aubergines, avocados, beetroot, carrots, cucumber, green beans, broad beans, celeriac, courgettes, fennel, garlic, mushrooms, onions, peppers, salad leaves and, of course, tomatoes (see opposite). Then there are dried vegetables – mushrooms, peppers and tomatoes – each of which can add an intense flavour to a dish. A risotto made with dried porcini mushrooms is a good example – see page 80.

Vine leaves

The young leaves of the grape vine are sold fresh in the Mediterranean and just need plunging in hot water for a few minutes to soften them before use. In this country they are likely to be sold in vacuum packs with brine, ready to be drained, rinsed well and dried before wrapping around a small amount of filling, as in Dolmades on page 30.

Vinegar

Vinegar can add a tang to salad dressings, mayonnaise (page 69) and sauces. In stews, a small amount of vinegar can be used in place of wine, while added to a marinade it can flavour fish and help to tenderise meat. The most appropriate varieties for Mediterranean cooking are wine vinegar (both red and white) and sherry vinegar. Keep a bottle of good-quality balsamic vinegar too – for dipping with bread and olive oil, for adding its mellow, sweet-sour flavour to salad dressings, and for sprinkling over fresh strawberries to enhance their flavour.

Wine

Wine, both red and white, features in savoury dishes such as risottos (try Mushroom Risotto on page 80) and many meat dishes (Slow-Cooked Beef in Red Wine on page 98 to name just one). In sweet dishes wine may be the liquid in which fruits are poached or it may form the basis of a jelly or an icy granita.

Yogurt

Yogurt has been used as an ingredient in Eastern European and Middle Eastern dishes for centuries. Some of the best Greek yogurt is made with the milk of sheep, though much is made with cow's milk. Whatever you choose, it needs to be thick and creamy with a good flavour. Yogurt is delicious served as a side dish or as part of an appetiser or starter. Serve it plain or flavoured with herbs and spices (as in Tsatsiki on page 28) or add it to salad dressings. When putting yogurt into a hot dish, such as a stew, stabilise it first to prevent it splitting (separating) by stirring in a little cornflour. Then add the yogurt-and-cornflour mixture to the hot dish before bringing it to the boil stirring all the while. Serve yogurt for dessert too – just as it is or drizzled with honey, with fresh or dried fruit, nuts, cakes and pastries.

2

APPETISERS, SOUPS & BREAD

For me, little typifies Mediterranean eating more than a table spread with a selection of little appetiser dishes. Indeed the Italian word *antipasto* literally means 'before the main course', *mezze* is the Greek or Turkish name for an array of small 'taster' plates, and *tapas* describes the delicacies served as hors d'oeuvres in Spain. They might comprise something as simple as a bowl of mixed olives and some fresh bread, with small basins of olive oil and balsamic vinegar for dipping, or some flat bread such as pitta with olive oil and an aromatic spice mix (see Dukkah on page 27). Then there are plates of wafer-thin salami and other cured meats that can be served just as they are or with sliced ripe melon, pear or fig. Or how about a platter of seafood such as smoked fish, squid rings and prawns still in their shells, with wedges of lemon or lime for squeezing over? Or a few jars of artichokes, sun-dried tomatoes and peppers, drained of the oil in which they have been stored? Or a spoonful of olive paste or green herb sauce (see pages 26 and 67) spread thickly on crisp toasts? The list goes on.

Soups feature prominently in Mediterranean cooking too. They can be light and delicate, ideal to begin a meal, or rich and stew-like, a meal in itself. They can be fast, with the freshest of ingredients being served in minutes, or slow, with long simmering and the last-minute addition of something fresh and vibrant – a little lemon juice perhaps, or a spoonful of pesto or anchovy paste (see pages 65 and 70).

Finally, let's not forget a basket of freshly made bread, without which a Mediterranean meal would seem incomplete.

Hummus

This version of the classic Middle Eastern dip is quick to make and uses less oil than usual. It's best prepared several hours in advance, or even the day before serving, to allow the flavour to develop. Make it as chunky or as smooth as you like and serve it as a starter with crusty bread or pitta bread, as part of a selection of dishes (mezze) or as a sandwich spread.

Serves 6

410g can chickpeas
1 garlic clove, roughly chopped
2 tbsp tahini (sesame paste)
3–4 tbsp Greek yogurt
3 tbsp fresh lemon juice
½ tsp ground cumin
1 tbsp extra virgin olive oil, plus extra to garnish
Freshly milled salt and black pepper
A little ground paprika, to garnish

1. Drain the chickpeas, reserving the liquid.

2. Put the chickpeas into a food processor or blender and add the remaining ingredients, except for the paprika. Blend until fairly smooth, scraping down the sides if necessary and adding about 2 tbsp of the reserved chickpea liquid to make a thick consistency.

3. Spoon into a serving dish, cover and chill until required.

4. To serve, drizzle a little extra oil over the surface of the hummus and sprinkle with a little paprika.

Baked Aubergine Purée

Here is my version of the Turkish dish called Baba Ghanoush. Serve it with warm pitta bread for dipping. The inclusion of the aubergine skins gives the purée a flecked appearance and a lovely 'smokey' flavour. If you prefer to omit them, at the end of step 1 put the hot aubergines into a plastic bag for 10–15 minutes to loosen the skins then split and scoop out the flesh. If you want to make a version with less oil, simply replace some of the olive oil with Greek yogurt in step 4.

Serves 4–6

2 medium aubergines
1 garlic clove, roughly chopped
2 tbsp fresh lemon or lime juice
½ tsp ground cumin
Freshly milled salt and black pepper
100ml/3½ fl oz extra virgin olive oil, plus extra to garnish
A few black olives, to garnish

1. Prick the aubergines with a fork and place them on a baking sheet. Put into a hot oven and cook at 200°C, fan 180°C, 400°F, gas 6, for 30–40 minutes or until quite soft.

2. Cut off and discard the aubergine stalks.

3. Put the aubergines into a food processor or blender and add the garlic, lemon juice, cumin and seasoning. Blend until smooth, scraping down the sides if necessary.

4. With the motor running, gradually add the oil.

5. Spoon the mixture into a serving bowl, cover and chill until required.

6. To serve, drizzle the top with a little extra oil and garnish with a few black olives.

Black Olive Paste

Based on Tapénade, the thick black olive and anchovy paste served in Provence. A small amount of cooked tuna is sometimes added. Serve with crudités (small sticks of raw vegetables) for dipping or as a spread on toasted slices of French bread. Also good served alongside grilled tuna, hard-boiled eggs or chicken.

Serves 6–8

150ml/¼ pt extra virgin olive oil
1 tsp lemon juice
1 tbsp brandy (optional)
200g/7 oz pitted black olives
3–4 anchovy fillets
1 garlic clove, roughly chopped
2 tbsp capers, rinsed and dried
Freshly milled black pepper

1. Put all the ingredients into a food processor or blender. Using the pulse button if possible, blend until finely chopped and as smooth as you like, scraping down the sides occasionally.
2. Spoon into a serving dish, cover and chill until required.

Green Olive Paste

Based on a traditional Italian mix. Serve with fresh Italian-style or French bread or spread it on toasted or griddled bread that has been rubbed with a cut garlic clove.

Serves 6–8

150ml/¼ pt extra virgin olive oil
200g/7 oz pitted green olives
1 garlic clove, roughly chopped
1 tbsp capers, rinsed and dried
2 tbsp ground almonds
½ tsp ground cumin
Freshly milled black pepper

1. Put all the ingredients into a food processor or blender. Using the pulse button if possible, blend until finely chopped and as smooth as you like, scraping down the sides occasionally.
2. Spoon into a serving dish, cover and chill until required.

Dukkah

This Egyptian dry spice blend has a wonderful combination of flavours. It's served as a snack or appetiser with small chunks of bread such as pitta – dunk the bread in a good-quality olive oil and then into the Dukkah. The mixture is also good sprinkled over freshly cooked vegetables, fish, chicken or meat. Store it in a tightly sealed container.

75g/2¾ oz hazelnuts or almonds
25g/1 oz sesame seeds
1 tbsp cumin seeds
1 tbsp coriander seeds
¼ tsp freshly milled salt
¼ tsp sugar
Freshly milled black pepper

1. Toast the nuts until golden brown and the skins begin to loosen – either under the grill or in a hot oven, taking care that they do not scorch. Put the hot nuts on to a clean cloth, gather it up to make a pouch and rub briskly so that any loose skins are removed (don't worry if they don't all come off). Discard the skins and chop the nuts finely – do this with a sharp knife on a board and not in a processor or similar machine or the nuts may get too pulverised and release their oils, making the mixture too moist to keep.

2. Toast the sesame seeds in the same way until light golden brown.

3. Crush the cumin and coriander seeds (with pestle and mortar or in a coffee grinder) until quite finely ground.

4. In a bowl, combine the spices, salt, sugar, seeds and nuts. Add a couple of twists of black pepper and mix well.

5. Once the mixture is completely cool, store it in an airtight container.

Yogurt and Cucumber Salad

Called Tsatsiki in Greece and Cacik in Turkey, this must be one of the most refreshing dishes to eat on a warm sunny day. Serve it as an appetiser with fresh crusty bread, or alongside grilled or barbecued meat (lamb and chicken in particular) or vegetable kebabs. It goes well with Keftethes (page 91) and Souvlaki (page 96). For best results, use thick yogurt and prepare it just before you want to serve it.

Serves 4–6

½ cucumber, grated
Freshly milled salt and pepper
200g carton Greek yogurt
1 tbsp extra virgin olive oil
2 tsp wine vinegar – white or red
1 garlic clove, crushed or finely chopped
2 tbsp chopped fresh mint or 1 tbsp dried

1. Put the grated cucumber into a colander or sieve and sprinkle with a little salt. Leave to drain for 1 hour.

2. Tip the yogurt into a large bowl and add the oil, vinegar, garlic and mint.

3. Scoop the cucumber up in your hand and gently squeeze out some of the liquid.

4. Stir the cucumber into the yogurt mixture, season to taste with salt and pepper and serve.

Tomato and Black Olive Tarts

These savoury puff-pastry tarts couldn't be easier to make. Use ready-rolled pastry and a jar of Tapénade (or you could make your own Black Olive Paste on page 26). Serve them as a snack or starter; or take them on your next picnic. Try other fillings too, such as tomato paste topped with crumbled feta cheese, olives and oregano; or pesto with cherry tomatoes, basil and pine nuts; or what about caramelised onions (as used in the French onion tart called Pissaladière on page 76) with anchovies and capers?

Makes 8

375g packet ready-rolled puff pastry, thawed if frozen
About 3 tbsp black olive paste
16 ripe cherry tomatoes
16 small fresh mint leaves
Sesame seeds

1. Preheat the oven to 200°C, fan 180°C, 400°F, gas 6.

2. Carefully unroll the puff pastry and, with a sharp knife, trim a thin strip off each side (this will help the pastry to puff up). Cut the pastry in half lengthways, and then cut each half crossways into four rectangles.

3. Put the pastry pieces on one large or two small baking sheets, leaving plenty of room between. (I usually line the baking sheets with non-stick baking paper first – it prevents the pastry sticking and keeps the baking sheets clean.)

4. Spread each rectangle with about 1 tsp black olive paste, leaving a border of pastry all round, and top with two tomatoes and two mint leaves. Sprinkle the tarts lightly with sesame seeds (over the pastry and the topping).

5. Put into the hot oven and cook for 10–15 minutes or until the pastry has puffed up around the edges and is crisp and golden brown.

6. Leave to cool slightly before serving.

Dolmades

Also called Dolmathes or Dolma, these stuffed vine leaves are based on a recipe given to me by a Greek couple who make award-winning wines on the slopes of the Sugar Loaf in Monmouthshire. Serve them warm, cold or at room temperature, as a starter or as part of a mezze (a selection of dishes served together). You could vary the ingredients by adding pine nuts, raisins, saffron or some crushed dried chilli in step 3.

Serves 6–8

225g/8 oz long grain rice
225g/8 oz vine leaves, fresh or packed in brine
1 medium onion, very finely chopped
3 medium tomatoes, finely chopped
1 tbsp tomato purée
2 tbsp finely chopped fresh parsley
2 tbsp dried crushed mint
¼ tsp ground cinnamon
¼ tsp ground allspice (optional)
Freshly milled salt and black pepper
2 tbsp olive oil
2 tomatoes, sliced
2 garlic cloves, cut into slivers
Juice of 1 lemon
3 tbsp dry white wine

1. Cook the rice in boiling water following the packet instructions. Drain, rinse in cold water and drain again.

2. If using fresh vine leaves, plunge them in boiling water until softened, drain and dry. Vine leaves in brine should be rinsed well and dried.

3. In a large bowl, put the rice, onion, chopped tomatoes, tomato purée, herbs and spices. Season and mix well.

4. Take a vine leaf, veins uppermost, and top with a small spoonful of the rice mixture. Roll up, folding in the sides, to make a cigar shape. Repeat with the remaining vine leaves and rice mixture.

5. Swirl the oil in the base of a large saucepan (a shallow one is best). Arrange the tomato slices in the oil – they will help to prevent the contents from sticking to the base of the pan. Tuck the stuffed vine leaves closely together in the pan, slipping garlic slivers between them and sprinkling lemon juice on each layer. Pour the wine over the top. Place a small plate over the parcels to hold them in place during cooking.

6. Cover securely with the lid and simmer very gently for about 2 hours, checking occasionally and adding a small amount of water each time the juices have been absorbed.

7. Remove from the heat and leave to cool. Once cool, remove the small plate. Now invert a large serving plate on the pan and quickly tip out the parcels with the tomato layer sitting on the top.

Falafel

Slip these chickpea croquettes into warmed-and-split pitta breads with some shredded crisp lettuce and a spoonful of Greek yogurt – wonderful. Then again, you could serve them as a starter on a small plate with a salad garnish and some mint-infused yogurt. Best results are obtained by using raw dried chickpeas that have been soaked overnight; using drained canned chickpeas usually results in croquettes that split open and do not cook well. Though the egg is an optional addition, it does help to bind the mixture.

Makes 18

250g/9 oz dried chickpeas, soaked overnight in plenty of cold water
1 medium onion, finely chopped
2 garlic cloves, chopped
3 tbsp chopped fresh parsley
3 tbsp chopped fresh coriander
1 tbsp ground cumin
2 tsp ground coriander
2 tbsp sesame seeds
½ tsp baking powder
½ tsp salt
A pinch each of freshly milled black pepper, cayenne and ground turmeric
1 medium egg, beaten (optional)
Oil for frying, such as sunflower or groundnut

1. Drain the chickpeas, put them into a food processor and buzz until roughly chopped. Add the remaining ingredients, except for the oil, and buzz until well ground, scraping down the sides of the processor bowl if necessary. Leave to stand for 30 minutes.

2. Shape the mixture into 18 balls.

3. Heat some oil in a frying pan (a depth of about 5mm/¼ inch is just about right), add six balls of the mixture at a time, flattening them slightly with a spatula, and cook for about 5 minutes on each side until crisp, golden brown and hot throughout.

4. Drain on kitchen paper and serve.

Green Lentil Soup

Lentil soups are served in most Mediterranean countries and vary from one place to the next. Serve this one with thick slices of garlicky bread, topped with a spoonful of crème fraîche, or sprinkled with crisp-fried pieces of bacon, pancetta or prosciutto.

Serves 6

1 tbsp olive oil
1 medium onion, finely chopped
½ tsp sugar
1 medium main-crop potato, chopped
1 garlic clove, finely chopped
250g/9 oz green lentils
1.5 litres/2¾ pt chicken stock
Freshly milled salt and pepper
2 tbsp chopped fresh herb, such as parsley or dill
2 tbsp balsamic vinegar

1. Put the oil, onion and sugar into a heavy-based saucepan and cook over medium heat for 5–10 minutes, stirring occasionally, until very soft and just beginning to turn golden.
2. Add the potato, garlic and lentils. Stir well then add the stock.
3. Bring to the boil then lower the heat, cover and simmer gently for 30–40 minutes, by which time the lentils should be very soft and tender.
4. Leave to cool slightly before tipping into a processor or blender (you may need to do this in batches) and buzzing until the soup is as smooth as you like (I prefer a fairly rough texture).
5. Return the mixture to the pan, adjust the seasoning to taste and stir in the herb and vinegar.
6. Reheat and serve.

To microwave:
1. Put the oil, onion and sugar into a large casserole and stir well. Cover and cook on HIGH for about 5 minutes or until soft, stirring once.
2. Add the potato, garlic and lentils. Stir well then add the (boiling) stock.
3. Bring to the boil on HIGH then simmer gently on MEDIUM or MED-LOW for 30–40 minutes, by which time the lentils should be very soft and tender.
4. Continue as for steps 4–5 above.
5. Reheat on HIGH, stirring occasionally, and serve.

White Bean, Squash and Tomato Soup

This beautiful soup always reminds me of warm, sunny climes. Choose your favourite squash – butternut, with its deep yellow flesh, is particularly good. The tomatoes can be skinned first if you like, although I don't usually bother.

Serves 4

1 tbsp olive oil
1 medium onion, finely chopped
1 garlic clove, finely chopped
500g/1 lb 2 oz squash (weighed after removing skin, seeds and fibres), cut into small cubes
250g/9 oz ripe tomatoes, finely chopped
400g can white beans, such as haricot or cannellini, drained
1.4 litres/2½ pt vegetable stock
Freshly milled salt and pepper
2 tbsp chopped fresh herb, such as mint or parsley

1. Put the oil and onion into a heavy-based saucepan and cook over medium heat for 5–10 minutes, stirring occasionally, until soft and golden brown.
2. Add the garlic, squash, tomatoes, beans and stock.
3. Bring to the boil then lower the heat and simmer gently for about 30 minutes, by which time the squash should be very soft and tender.
4. Ladle about one third of the mixture into a processor or blender and buzz until smooth.
5. Return the mixture to the pan contents, adjust the seasoning to taste and stir in the herb.
6. Reheat and serve.

To microwave:

1. Put the oil and onion into a large casserole and stir well. Cover and cook on HIGH for about 5 minutes or until soft, stirring once.
2. Add the garlic, squash, tomatoes, beans and (boiling) stock.
3. Bring to the boil on HIGH then simmer gently on MEDIUM or MED-LOW for about 30 minutes, by which time the squash should be very soft and tender.
4. Continue as for steps 4–5 above.
5. Reheat on HIGH, stirring occasionally, and serve.

Fennel, Chickpea and Bean Soup

I have been known to make this soup with fennel that has bolted in my garden – just lots and lots of fronds – and it still tastes delicious.

Serves 4

2 tbsp olive oil
1 medium onion, finely chopped
2 fennel bulbs, thinly sliced
2 garlic cloves, finely chopped
400g can chickpeas, including the liquid
300ml/½ pt vegetable stock
1 chicken stock cube
Freshly milled salt and pepper
400g can white beans, such as cannellini or haricot, drained

1. Put the oil and onion into a heavy-based saucepan and cook over medium heat for 5–10 minutes, stirring occasionally, until soft but not browned.
2. Stir in the fennel and garlic then add the chickpeas and their liquid, vegetable stock and the stock cube. Season with pepper.
3. Bring to the boil then lower the heat and simmer gently for about 30 minutes, by which time the fennel should be very soft and tender.
4. Leave to cool slightly before tipping into a processor or blender (you may need to do this in batches) and buzzing until the soup is as smooth as you like (I prefer a fairly rough texture).
5. Return the mixture to the pan, adjust the seasoning to taste and stir in the drained beans.
6. Reheat and serve.

To microwave:
1. Put the oil and onion into a large casserole and stir well. Cover and cook on HIGH for about 5 minutes or until soft, stirring once.
2. Stir in the fennel and garlic then add the chickpeas and their liquid, (boiling) vegetable stock and the stock cube. Season with pepper.
3. Bring to the boil on HIGH then simmer gently on MEDIUM or MED-LOW for about 30 minutes, by which time the fennel should be very soft and tender.
4. Continue as for steps 4–5 above.
5. Reheat on HIGH, stirring occasionally, and serve.

Gazpacho

Gazpacho is a refreshing summer soup that hails from southern Spain. It needs no cooking, is made in minutes with a food processor or blender and is served chilled with crisp croûtons floating on top.

Serves 4–6

550g/1¼ lb ripe tomatoes, skin and seeds removed, chopped
1 small cucumber, skin and seeds removed, chopped
160g jar roasted peppers, drained and chopped
1 celery stick, thinly sliced
6 spring onions, sliced
2 garlic cloves, crushed
2 tbsp extra virgin olive oil
2 tbsp red or white wine vinegar
115g/4 oz fresh white breadcrumbs (I like to use ciabatta)
2 tsp sugar
Freshly milled salt and black pepper
600ml/1 pt cold chicken stock, plus extra if necessary

1. Put the tomatoes into a large bowl and add the cucumber, peppers, celery, onions, garlic, oil, vinegar, breadcrumbs and sugar. Season with salt and pepper and stir well. Cover and leave to stand for 10–15 minutes, stirring once or twice.

2. Stir in the cold stock.

3. Tip into the blender (in batches) and blend until smooth.

4. If necessary, add extra stock until the consistency of the soup is perfect for serving, then chill for 2 hours or more.

Tomato, Bean and Artichoke Soup

A soup that is made from store-cupboard ingredients can bring a sunny Mediterranean feel to a winter's day.

Serves 4–6

2 tbsp olive oil
1 medium onion, finely chopped
1 garlic clove, finely chopped
400g can tomatoes
420g can white beans, such as haricot, cannellini or butter beans, drained
400g can artichoke hearts, drained and quartered
1 tbsp chopped fresh thyme or oregano or 1 tsp dried
850ml/1½ pt chicken or vegetable stock
Freshly milled salt and black pepper
Chopped fresh parsley

1. Put the oil and onion into a heavy-based saucepan and cook over medium heat for 5–10 minutes, stirring occasionally, until soft but not browned.

2. Stir in the remaining ingredients except the parsley.

3. Bring to the boil, then lower the heat and simmer gently for about 30 minutes.

4. Adjust the seasoning to taste before serving sprinkled with parsley.

To microwave:
1. Put the oil and onion into a large casserole and stir well. Cover and cook on HIGH for about 5 minutes or until soft, stirring once.

2. Stir in the remaining ingredients (it's best to add the stock hot) except the parsley.

3. Bring to the boil on HIGH then simmer gently on MEDIUM or MED-LOW for about 30 minutes.

4. Adjust the seasoning to taste before serving sprinkled with parsley.

Mediterranean Fish Soup

Fish soup of one form or another is served all over the Mediterranean. This one lies somewhere between a soup and a stew. Choose your favourite fish or whatever is in season – check the list on page 12. Though it is delicious served just as it is with plenty of fresh crusty bread or toast, Aioli on page 70 or Rouille on page 68 makes the dish more special.

Serves 4–6

2 tbsp olive oil
1 large onion, finely chopped
2 garlic cloves, finely chopped
1 medium carrot, finely chopped
1 medium leek, thinly sliced
400g can chopped tomatoes
600ml/1 pt fish stock
1 tsp dried thyme
Strip of orange zest
2 bay leaves
About 800g/1¾ lb mixed fish (skinless fish fillet, cut into bite-size pieces, raw cockles and mussels in their shells)
115g/4 oz peeled prawns
Freshly milled salt and pepper

1. Heat a large pan and add the oil, onion, garlic, carrot and leek. Cook gently for about 10 minutes, stirring occasionally, or until soft.

2. Add the tomatoes, stock, thyme, orange zest and bay leaves. Bring to the boil, cover and simmer for 10 minutes.

3. Add all the fish, cover and simmer very gently for about 5 minutes or until the fish is cooked and the shells have opened.

4. Season to taste and serve, discarding the bay leaves.

To microwave:
1. Put the oil into a very large casserole and add the onion, garlic, carrot and leek. Cover and cook on HIGH for 5 minutes, stirring once or twice, until very soft.

2. Stir in the tomatoes, stock, thyme, orange zest and bay leaves. Cover and cook on HIGH for about 5 minutes, or until the mixture comes to the boil. Cook on MEDIUM for 5 minutes.

3. Stir in all the fish, cover and cook on MEDIUM for about 5 minutes or until the fish is cooked and the shells have opened.

4. Season to taste and serve, discarding the bay leaves.

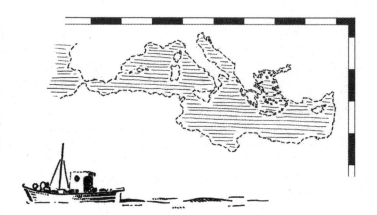

Bruschetta

Bruschetta, this Italian toast flavoured with a hint of garlic and olive oil, is perfect for relaxed occasions when you want to rustle up some food for friends while you all chat in the kitchen. Serve it plain and simple or with a savoury topping. Bruschetta is best made with good crusty bread that is at least two days old. Slice the bread about 1cm/½ in thick and toast until slightly charred – a griddle pan produces the best results for me, otherwise use a heavy-based frying pan or a hot grill. While the toast is hot, rub one side with a cut clove of garlic and drizzle over some extra virgin olive oil. Serve it just as it is or add one of the toppings below, piling the mixture on to the warm toast and serving immediately.

Toppings:
Olive paste, page 26.
Salsa Verde, page 67.
Anchoiade, page 70.
Artichokes in oil, drained and quartered.
Peeled and chopped ripe tomatoes, chopped garlic and pitted black olives.
Caramelised onions with herbs, like the ones used to top Pissaladière on page 76.
Drain and flake a 200g can tuna and mix with 6 tbsp mayonnaise, 4 chopped anchovy fillets, 1 tbsp chopped capers, the juice of a small lemon and some chopped fresh parsley.
A mixture of soft roasted vegetables tossed in olive oil and a little lemon juice – try red onions, peppers, courgettes, aubergine and cherry tomatoes.
Strips of grilled red or yellow peppers tossed in a little balsamic vinegar, or try Roasted Pepper Salad on page 52.
Mushrooms browned in olive oil with finely chopped garlic and some chopped fresh herbs.
Tiny salad leaves, such as rocket and grated Parmesan cheese.
Thin slices of cured ham topped with mozzarella or goat's cheese and grilled until bubbling.
Roughly chopped walnuts topped with soft goat's cheese and grilled.

Pizza Dough

It hardly seems worth reducing the quantity to make just one pizza when you can roll out and freeze one or two more ready for another occasion. If you have a bread machine, simply put all the ingredients into the pan (in the order recommended by the manufacturer) and select the PIZZA, QUICK DOUGH or DOUGH setting.

Makes 2 or 3 large pizzas

500g/1 lb 2 oz strong white bread flour
1 tsp salt
1 tsp Easybake yeast
2 tbsp olive oil

1.   Put the flour into a large bowl and stir in the salt and yeast. Make a well in the centre and add the oil and 300ml/½ pt tepid water (an easy way to do this is to measure 200ml cold water then making it up to the full quantity with boiling water). Stir well, making sure all the flour is mixed in before tipping the dough out on to a lightly floured surface.

2.   Knead the mixture until smooth and elastic (this will take about 10 minutes).

3.   Put it into a lightly oiled bowl, cover with oiled film and leave in a warm place for about 1 hour until doubled in size.

4.   Tip the risen dough out on to the floured surface and knead again (knocking out the air) for a minute or two until smooth. The dough is now ready to roll out.

5.   Using a rolling pin or your hands, roll or push the dough out into two or three circles. Put the pizza base(s) on to lightly oiled baking trays. (At this stage, the dough can be frozen.)

6.   Preheat the oven to 200°C, fan 180°C, 400°F, gas 6.

7.   Spread the pizzas with a thin layer of tomato sauce (see pages 68 and 66) or passata (sieved tomatoes), leaving the edges free.

8.   Scatter your chosen toppings (see overleaf) over the tomato and drizzle the edges of the dough with a little olive oil.

9.   Put into the hot oven and cook for about 15 minutes until the edges are puffed up and crisp, the toppings are golden brown and the pizza base is cooked through.

Try these toppings:

- ❖ Torn basil leaves, a few baby plum tomato halves, slices of mozzarella and a drizzle of olive oil.

- ❖ Black olives, drained anchovy fillets, sliced mozzarella and a drizzle of olive oil.

- ❖ Drained canned artichokes in oil (quartered), capers and freshly grated Parmesan cheese.

- ❖ Roasted or fried red onion wedges, crumbled goat's cheese and pine nuts.

- ❖ Thinly sliced tomatoes, fresh thyme leaves and slices of Parma ham, all drizzled with olive oil.

- ❖ Grilled vegetables (such as slices of red or yellow pepper, courgettes and aubergines) topped with fresh thyme leaves and slices of Mozzarella cheese.

- ❖ Thinly sliced chorizo or other spicy sausage, chopped fresh rosemary and freshly grated Parmesan cheese.

- ❖ Lightly fried mushroom slices, oregano leaves (fresh or dried), green olives and flakes of cheese (mozzarella, Parmesan or goat's).

Pitta Bread

These flatbreads are popular throughout the Middle East. When split, they have a natural pocket that's ideal for filling with salad, vegetables, meat, kebabs or falafel. They can also be served warm or toasted with mezze or with dips such as extra virgin olive oil, balsamic vinegar or hummus (page 24). If you have a bread machine, simply put all the ingredients into the pan (in the order recommended by the manufacturer) and select the PIZZA, QUICK DOUGH or DOUGH setting.

Makes 12

500g/1 lb 2 oz strong white bread flour
1 tsp fine sea salt
1 tsp Easybake yeast
1 tbsp olive oil

1. Put the flour into a large bowl and stir in the salt and yeast. Make a well in the centre and add the oil and 300ml/½ pt tepid water (an easy way to do this is to measure 200ml cold water then making it up to the full quantity with boiling water). Stir well, making sure all the flour is mixed in before tipping the dough out on to a lightly floured surface.

2. Knead the mixture until smooth and elastic (this will take about 10 minutes).

3. Put it into a lightly oiled bowl, cover with oiled film and leave in a warm place for about 1 hour until doubled in size.

4. Turn the risen dough on to the floured surface and knead lightly, knocking out the air, for a minute or two until smooth.

5. Divide the mixture into 12 equal pieces and shape each one into a ball. Place on the floured surface, cover with a dry cloth and leave to rest for 10 minutes (after which it should roll out more easily).

6. With a floured rolling pin, roll out each ball into an oval or circle about 15cm/6 in wide and 0.5cm/¼ in thick. Place on the floured surface, cover with the cloth and leave to rise for 20–30 minutes.

7. Meanwhile, put two or three baking trays in the oven and preheat to 240°C, fan 220°C, 475°F, gas 9. (A fan oven produces the best results for me.)

8. Transfer some of the dough pieces on to one hot baking tray. Bake for about 3 minutes or until puffed up and cooked, but not browned.

9. Take them out of the oven and leave on a wire rack to cool slightly before covering with a dry cloth (to keep the crust soft) and leaving to cool.

10. Cook the remaining dough pieces in the same way.

Focaccia

Serve this Italian bread warm, split and filled with roast vegetables, ham, salami, cheese, olives and so on; or just as it is with soups or salads. Focaccia reheats well too – just wrap it in foil and pop it into a really hot oven for about 10 minutes. If you have a bread machine, put all the ingredients into the pan (in the order recommended by the manufacturer) and select the PIZZA, QUICK DOUGH or DOUGH setting.

500g/1 lb 2 oz strong white bread flour
1 tsp fine sea salt
1 tsp Easybake yeast
5 tbsp olive oil, plus extra
Semolina
2 generous tsp freeze-dried herbs, such as oregano and rosemary
Sea salt flakes

1. Put the flour into a large bowl and stir in the salt and yeast. Make a well in the centre and add 2 tbsp oil and about 300ml/½ pt tepid water (an easy way to do this is to measure 200ml cold water then making it up to the full quantity with boiling water). Stir well, making sure all the flour is mixed in before tipping the dough out on to a lightly floured surface.

2. Knead the mixture until smooth and elastic (this will take about 10 minutes).

3. Put it into a lightly oiled bowl, cover with oiled film and leave in a warm place for about 1 hour until doubled in size.

4. Turn the risen dough on to the floured surface and knead lightly, knocking out the air, for a minute or two until smooth.

5. Using a rolling pin or your hands, roll or push the dough out into a rough oval or rectangular shape about 1.5cm/½ in thick (this may need patience and perseverance because the dough tends to shrink back again).

6. Dust a baking tray with semolina and place the dough on top. Drizzle the remaining 3 tbsp oil as evenly as you can over the top and sprinkle with the herbs. Using your fingers on one hand, make lots of deep indents all over the dough.

7. Leave to rise in a warm place until the dough has doubled in height.

8. Put into a hot oven at 220°C, fan 200°C, 425°F, gas 7, and bake for about 15 minutes until golden brown and cooked through.

9. Take the bread out of the oven, drizzle extra olive oil over the top and sprinkle with a light covering of sea salt flakes.

10. Leave to cool on a wire rack.

Olive Bread

Make Focaccia as above, scattering black or green olives (or a mixture) over the dough in step 6. Just before baking, gently push the olives down into the risen dough so that they lie just below, or level with, the surface.

Flatbreads

These Middle Eastern flatbreads should be crisp and dry on the bottom and soft and slightly chewy on top. When pieces are torn off, warm air pockets are revealed inside. Use them for mopping up sauce on the plate or for serving with dips. Serve them warm, straight out of the oven, before they cool completely. If you do need to make them in advance, reheat them by sprinkling lightly with water and popping them into a hot oven for a couple of minutes only. To make the dough in a bread machine, put all the ingredients into the pan (in the order recommended by the manufacturer) and select the PIZZA, QUICK DOUGH or DOUGH setting.

Makes 8

500g/1 lb 2 oz strong white bread flour
1 tsp fine sea salt
1 tsp Easybake yeast
2 tbsp olive oil
Beaten egg
Seeds such as sesame, nigella, poppy, or a mixture

1. Put the flour into a large bowl and stir in the salt and yeast. Make a well in the centre and add the oil and about 300ml/½ pt tepid water (an easy way to do this is to measure 200ml cold water then making it up to the full quantity with boiling water). Stir well, making sure all the flour is mixed in before tipping the dough out on to a lightly floured surface.

2. Knead the mixture until smooth and elastic (this will take about 10 minutes).

3. Put it into a lightly oiled bowl, cover with oiled film and leave in a warm place for about 1 hour until doubled in size.

4. Meanwhile, remove the oven shelves (to prevent burns as you lean into the hot oven) and put a large baking tray on the bottom of the oven or, if this is not possible, the bottom shelf. Preheat to 240°C, fan 220°C, 475°F, gas 9. (A fan oven produces the best results for me.)

5. Turn the risen dough on to the floured surface and knead lightly, knocking out the air, for a minute or two until smooth.

6. Divide the mixture into eight equal pieces and shape each one into a ball. Place on the floured surface, cover with a dry cloth and leave to rest for 10 minutes (to make rolling out easier).

7. With a rolling pin, roll one piece of dough out thinly until it measures about 20cm/8 in. Repeat with the second piece. Brush their tops with beaten egg and sprinkle some seeds over.

8. Transfer them carefully to the hot baking tray in the oven and bake for 3–5 minutes until puffed up, cooked and only just beginning to colour around the edges. While they are cooking, quickly roll out the next two.

9. Remove from the oven and wrap gently in a dry cloth, adding the rest as they come out of the oven.

3

SALADS, SIDE DISHES & SAUCES

Just where appetisers end and salads and sides dishes start is difficult to determine. With this in mind, this chapter is simply an extension of the previous one, for the dishes are decidedly interchangeable and many of them would make wonderful light meals too.

It takes just a few ingredients to rustle up a salad – like roasted vegetables tossed with a splash of vinegar, perhaps with some couscous, rice or pasta stirred in. Next time you mix a basic salad with lettuce leaves, cucumber slices and tomato wedges, consider customising it – Niçoise style might include red onion rings, cooked green beans, flaked tuna and slices of hard-boiled egg; while a Greek salad might have cubes of salty feta cheese, red pepper and black olives scattered with oregano. Make the most of seasonal young vegetables too, by lightly boiling or steaming them whole and drizzling with olive oil and fresh lemon juice. Or open a selection of canned beans and add some thin rings of red onion, olive oil and wine vinegar.

Side dishes, those that might be served alongside fish, meat or poultry, are often best kept simple. Try a bowl of lightly cooked vegetables such as broad beans or green beans and turn them in a little olive oil and plenty of black pepper. Or serve a selection of grilled vegetables tossed in oil with a splash of wine vinegar. Or a salad of oranges and olives drizzled with olive oil and seasoned with freshly milled salt and pepper.

And finally to sauces, where you will find some of my favourites – nothing fancy, just a variety of textures, vibrant colours and exciting flavours, and all very easy to make.

Tabbouleh

Serve this Lebanese salad as part of a mezze with tiny leaves of crisp lettuce to scoop it up, as a starter with crusty bread or as a side dish with grilled fish, chicken or meat.

Serves 4

85g/3 oz bulgur wheat
A good handful of flat-leaf parsley, about 85g/3 oz, stalks removed
A small handful of mint leaves, about 50g/1¾ oz
4 tbsp extra virgin olive oil
Juice of 1 large lemon
Freshly milled salt and pepper
225g/8 oz ripe tomatoes, cut into small dice
6 spring onions, finely chopped

1. Pour cold water over the bulgur wheat to cover it and leave to stand for 15 minutes.

2. Meanwhile, finely chop the herbs. Whisk the oil with the lemon juice and season well with salt and pepper.

3. Drain the wheat, squeezing the grains to remove excess water, and put it into a large bowl.

4. Pour the oil-and-lemon dressing over it and mix well. Stir in the tomatoes and then the remaining ingredients.

5. Leave to stand for at least 30 minutes to allow the flavours to intermingle before serving.

Italian Bread Salad

In Italy this salad is called Panzanella. Be sure to use ciabatta that is two or three days old and don't be tempted to use ordinary (British) bread. For good flavour, make sure the tomatoes are ripe and tasty and the olive oil is the best quality, and make it no sooner than about 45 minutes before you want to serve it. Here is the basic recipe to which you could add any mixture of extra ingredients such as capers, chopped red chillies, pitted black olives and slivers of sun-dried tomatoes. Sometimes I crisp the bread first, either by baking it in a hot oven until dry and golden brown or by browning it in a little olive oil.

Serves 6 as a starter or side salad

6 thick slices from a 2–3 day-old ciabatta loaf, torn into small pieces
675g/1½ lb ripe tomatoes, roughly chopped
1 red onion, thinly sliced
2 garlic cloves, finely chopped
Generous handful of fresh basil leaves
6 tbsp extra virgin olive oil
3 tbsp red wine vinegar
Freshly milled salt and black pepper
Flakes of Parmesan cheese, to serve

1. Put the bread into a large bowl and add the tomatoes, onion, garlic and basil.

2. Whisk together the oil, vinegar and seasoning.

3. Pour the oil-and-vinegar dressing over the salad and toss gently until combined.

4. Serve topped with flakes of Parmesan cheese.

Potato and Chilli Salad

Similar salads are served all over the Mediterranean. Remember that chillies vary in their strength so please adjust the quantity to suit your taste. Serve the salad warm or cold and, if the mood takes you, throw in thin slices of spicy sausage, such as chorizo, or some chopped spring onions.

Serves 4

500g/1 lb 2 oz small salad potatoes
2 tbsp olive oil, plus extra if necessary
1 garlic clove, finely chopped
1 red chilli, seeds removed and finely chopped
Freshly milled salt and pepper
2 tbsp chopped fresh parsley

1. Cook the potatoes in boiling water for 15–20 minutes until just tender. Drain and cut into thick slices.

2. Put the oil into a large non-stick frying pan and add the garlic and chilli. Cook over medium heat, stirring frequently, until soft and just beginning to brown.

3. Remove the pan from the heat and stir in the potatoes, tossing them well and adding extra olive oil if wished.

4. Season with salt and pepper and scatter the parsley over the top.

To microwave:
1. Put the potatoes into a large casserole with 4 tbsp water. Cover and cook on HIGH for about 10 minutes, stirring occasionally, until tender. Drain and cut into thick slices.

2. Put the oil into a large bowl and add the garlic and chilli. Cook on HIGH for 30–45 seconds until soft.

3. As steps 3 and 4 above.

Roasted Pepper Salad

Versions of this salad crop up in several Mediterranean countries. This one has been kept simple and is delicious just as it is, served at room temperature. Feel free to add extra ingredients though, such as one or more of the following: finely chopped garlic, anchovies, capers, olives, chopped fresh herbs or toasted pine nuts.

Serves about 6

8 red or yellow peppers, or a mixture of both
3 tbsp extra virgin olive oil
2 tsp red wine vinegar
Freshly milled salt and pepper

1. Put the peppers into a roasting tin and cook at 240°C, fan 220°C, 475°F, gas 9, for about 30 minutes, turning them over at least once, until soft and the skins are blistered and blackened. Carefully tip the peppers into a thick freezer bag and leave to stand (this helps loosen the skins).

2. Balance a large sieve over a bowl.

3. When the peppers are cool enough to handle, tip them into the sieve. Take a pepper and, holding it over the sieve, remove the skin and seeds, allowing any juice to drip back into the bowl. Repeat with the remaining peppers.

4. Cut the pepper flesh into strips and put into a serving dish.

5. Using a whisk, mix the pepper juices with the olive oil and vinegar. Season very lightly with salt and pepper. Pour the mixture over the pepper strips and chill until required.

6. If possible, allow the salad to return to room temperature before serving.

Cinnamon-Scented Couscous with Onions, Fruit and Pine Nuts

This recipe conjures up Mediterranean flavours that are warm, fragrant and sweet. It's delicious served hot with lamb or chicken or at room temperature as part of a buffet table.

Serves 6–8

3 tbsp pine nuts
2 tbsp olive oil
2 medium onions, thinly sliced
1 tsp sugar
250g/9 oz couscous
3 generous tbsp raisins or chopped ready-to-eat apricots
1 tsp ground cinnamon
400ml/14 fl oz boiling vegetable stock

1. Heat the pine nuts in a frying pan, shaking occasionally, until golden brown. Tip into a large bowl.

2. Pour 1 tbsp oil into the frying pan, add the onions and sugar and cook over low-medium heat, stirring occasionally, until very soft and golden brown. Add to the pine nuts.

3. Stir the couscous, fruit and cinnamon into the onion mixture. Add the remaining 1 tbsp olive oil. Pour the boiling stock over, stir well and leave to stand for 5–10 minutes.

Couscous with Carrot and Mint Dressing

Take couscous and carrots, add fresh mint leaves, olive oil, stock, lemon and sesame seeds. Result? A refreshing salad, made in minutes, that can be served warm or at room temperature, with or without accompaniments. Although the toasted sesame seeds are optional, they do add a wonderful flavour to the dish.

Serves 6–8

250g/9 oz couscous
2 medium carrots (about 300g/10½ oz) finely grated
3 tbsp olive oil
2 tbsp lemon juice
About 15g/½ oz mint leaves, finely chopped
2 tbsp sesame seeds, toasted (optional)
400ml/14 fl oz boiling vegetable stock
Freshly milled salt and black pepper

1. Put the couscous into a large bowl with the carrots, oil, lemon juice, mint and sesame seeds (if using). Stir well.

2. Pour over the boiling vegetable stock and stir well. Leave to stand for at least 10 minutes before adjusting the seasoning to taste.

Lentil and Rice Salad

Another quick-to-make salad. Delicious served warm or at room temperature, with or without accompaniments.

Serves 6–8

250g/9 oz long-grain rice
1 tsp dried oregano
410g can lentils, drained
2 tbsp balsamic vinegar
5 tbsp olive oil
3 tbsp finely chopped fresh mint
3 tbsp finely chopped fresh parsley
Freshly milled salt and pepper

1. Cook the rice (on the hob or in the microwave) following packet instructions, adding the oregano to the boiling water. Drain.

2. Stir the remaining ingredients into the drained hot rice and leave to cool.

Spiced Apricots with Cheese

Start preparing this salad two days before it is to be eaten. The salty taste of feta cheese goes well in this dish. You could of course omit the cheese altogether and serve the apricots to accompany cold roast meat and chicken, smoked fish and meat (smoked duck is particularly good), cured meat and spicy sausages.

Serves 4

225g/8 oz dried apricots (not the ready-to-eat variety)
1 small lemon
150ml/¼ pt red wine vinegar
100ml/4 fl oz runny honey
1 cinnamon stick
8 black peppercorns
200g packet feta cheese, drained and cut into small cubes
Salad leaves to serve
Chives to garnish

1. Two days before serving, put the apricots into a bowl, cover them with boiling water and leave to stand overnight to plump up.
2. Next day, cut the zest from the lemon in strips, making sure the white pith is left behind (a potato peeler is handy for this job). Drain the apricots.
3. Put the vinegar into a pan and add the honey, lemon zest, cinnamon and peppercorns. Bring to the boil while stirring.
4. Add the drained apricots, bring back to the boil, then simmer gently for about 5 minutes.
5. Spoon the mixture into a dish (not metal), cover and leave at room temperature for several hours or overnight.
6. To serve, drain the apricots (reserving the juice) and toss with the feta cheese. Pile the mixture on to salad leaves, snip some chives over the top and drizzle with a little of the liquid from the apricots.

To microwave:
1. Follow steps 1 and 2 above.
2. Put the vinegar into a casserole and add the honey, lemon zest, cinnamon and peppercorns. Cover and microwave on HIGH for about 2 minutes or until boiling.
3. Add the drained apricots and cook, uncovered for 6–7 minutes, stirring occasionally.
4. Continue with steps 5 and 6 above.

Peperonata

This Italian dish can be served hot to accompany meat or fish, or cold as part of a selection of starters or salads. It's one of those dishes that reheats very well, almost improving in its texture and flavour as it does so.

Serves 6

4 tbsp olive oil
2 medium onions, thinly sliced
2 garlic cloves, finely chopped
2 large red peppers, seeds removed, cut into strips
2 large yellow peppers, seeds removed, cut into strips
400g can chopped tomatoes
Freshly milled salt and black pepper

1. Put the oil, onions and garlic into a large pan and cook over medium heat for 10–15 minutes, stirring occasionally, until soft and lightly browned.

2. Stir in the peppers and cook, stirring occasionally, for a few minutes.

3. Add the tomatoes and seasoning. Bring to the boil then lower the heat, cover and simmer gently for 30–40 minutes, stirring now and again, until the peppers are very soft. If you like, remove the cover for the final 10 minutes of cooking so that the juices reduce slightly.

To microwave:
1. Put the oil, onions and garlic into a large casserole, cover and cook on HIGH for 10 minutes, stirring occasionally, until very soft.

2. Stir in the peppers, cover and cook for 5 minutes.

3. Stir in the tomatoes and seasoning. Bring to the boil on HIGH then cook on MEDIUM for 20–30 minutes, stirring occasionally, until the peppers are very soft.

4. To reduce the sauce, remove the cover and continue cooking on MEDIUM for about 10 minutes.

Ratatouille

Ratatouille originates in the Provence region of France. Auber-
gines, courgettes, peppers, onions, tomatoes and garlic are
cooked gently in olive oil. It reheats quite happily. Serve hot, cold
or at room temperature.

Serves 4–6

5 tbsp olive oil
2 large onions, thinly sliced
1 clove garlic, crushed
1 green pepper, seeds removed, thinly sliced
1 tsp sugar
3 medium aubergines, thinly sliced
2–3 courgettes, thinly sliced
4–6 tomatoes, skinned and quartered
Salt and black pepper
Bouquet garni

1. Heat the oil in a large frying pan, add the onions, garlic, pepper and sugar, cover and cook for about 8 minutes, stirring occasionally, until soft but not brown.

2. Stir in the aubergines, courgettes, tomatoes, seasoning and bouquet garni. Cover and cook gently for 30 minutes, stirring occasionally until all the vegetables are soft.

3. Remove the bouquet garni before serving.

Vegetable Couscous with Chilli and Lemon

Adapt this by varying the vegetables and herb according to the season. If you decide to use artichokes in oil (in place of canned) you may want to omit the final tablespoon of oil in step 4. It's good with grilled fish or meat and it makes a great salad in its own right. For a more substantial dish, serve it topped with thinly sliced red onion, cubes of feta or mozzarella and a few black olives.

Serves 6–8

3 tbsp olive oil
2 medium leeks, thinly sliced
2 celery sticks, thinly sliced
1 medium carrot, thinly sliced
1 garlic clove, finely chopped
250g/9 oz couscous
400g can artichokes, drained and quartered lengthways
1 red chilli, seeds removed and thinly sliced
Finely grated rind of 1 lemon
600ml/1 pt vegetable stock
Juice of ½ lemon (about 2 tbsp)
Freshly milled salt and pepper (optional)
3 tbsp chopped fresh coriander leaves

1. Put 2 tbsp oil into a large, heavy-based casserole and stir in the leeks, celery and carrot. Cover and cook over medium heat for 10–15 minutes, stirring occasionally, until soft but not browned.
2. Stir in the garlic followed by the couscous then the artichokes, chilli and lemon rind. Add the stock and lemon juice.
3. Bring just to the boil then remove from the heat, cover and leave to stand for 10–12 minutes until the couscous has absorbed all the liquid.
4. Season lightly if necessary and gently stir in the remaining 1 tbsp oil and the coriander.

To microwave:
1. Put 2 tbsp oil into a large casserole and stir in the leeks, celery and carrot. Cover and cook on HIGH for about 10 minutes, stirring once or twice, until very soft.
2. As step 2 above, using hot stock.
3. Cover and cook on HIGH for 2 minutes then leave to stand, covered, for 10–12 minutes until the couscous has absorbed all the liquid.
4. As step 4 above.

Chickpea Fritters

These golden fritters, called Panisses in Provence, are made with chickpea flour, which is also known as besan or gram flour. Their texture is lovely – crisp on the outside and creamy soft inside. Serve them just as they are with vegetable or meat dishes (such as Slow-Cooked Beef in Red Wine on page 98) or sprinkled with sugar for dessert (omit the pepper if you like and use only a small pinch of salt). Traditionally, they are deep-fried; here, they are crisped in a little hot oil in a frying pan and, to my mind, taste just as good.

Makes about 32 small triangles

250g/9 oz chickpea flour
Freshly milled salt and black pepper
Oil for frying

1. Sift the flour into a large saucepan and season with a little salt and pepper. Using a whisk, stir in 1 litre/1¾ pt cold water. Stir until well mixed.

2. Heat, stirring, until the mixture thickens and comes to the boil. Lower the heat and continue stirring and cooking gently for about 5 minutes. (Take care, the mixture is likely to spit – you may want to cover your stirring hand with a cloth.)

3. Tip the mixture into a shallow baking tray measuring about 30cm/12 in square. Spread the mixture evenly and level the surface. Leave until cold and firm.

4. When cold, cut into triangles (or squares, rectangles or circles).

5. Heat some oil in a frying pan and cook the fritters until golden brown on both sides.

6. Drain on kitchen paper then serve.

To microwave:

1. Sift the flour into a large casserole and season with a little salt and pepper. Using a whisk, stir in 1 litre/1¾ pt cold water. Stir until well mixed.

2. Microwave, uncovered, on HIGH for about 10 minutes until the mixture thickens and just comes to the boil. (Whisk well two or three times during this time to prevent lumps forming.) Reduce the microwave power to MEDIUM and continue cooking for a further 5 minutes, stirring once or twice.

3. Continue as in steps 3–6 above.

Fennel and Tomato Gratin

Especially good served alongside grilled fish, chicken or sausages. Alternatively, serve just as it is with some crusty bread to mop up the sauce.

Serves 4

2 large fennel bulbs
2 tbsp olive oil
400g can whole plum tomatoes
Finely grated rind and juice of ½ lemon
2 tsp sugar
200ml/7 fl oz vegetable stock
Freshly milled salt and black pepper
4 tbsp freshly grated Parmesan cheese
3 tbsp fresh breadcrumbs

1. Trim the fennel and cut in half lengthways, keeping the base intact if possible. Cut each half, lengthways again, into four or five wedges.

2. Put the oil in a shallow pan and add the fennel. Cover and cook quickly, turning occasionally, until golden brown.

3. Add the tomatoes, lemon rind and juice, sugar and stock. Bring to the boil, cover and simmer gently for about 15 minutes until the fennel is just tender.

4. Remove the lid, increase the heat and bubble rapidly for about 10 minutes until the sauce has reduced and thickened slightly. Season to taste with salt and pepper.

5. Spoon the mixture into a shallow flameproof dish. Combine the Parmesan and breadcrumbs and scatter over the top.

6. Put under a hot grill until bubbling and golden brown.

To microwave:

1. As step 1 opposite.

2. Put the oil in a large casserole and stir in the fennel. Cover and cook on HIGH for 5 minutes, stirring once.

3. Add the tomatoes, lemon rind and juice, sugar and (hot) stock. Cover and cook on HIGH until the mixture comes to the boil, then lower the power to MEDIUM and cook for about 15 minutes, stirring once or twice, until the fennel is just tender.

4. Uncover and cook on HIGH for about 10 minutes, stirring occasionally, until the sauce has reduced and thickened slightly.

5. As steps 5 and 6 opposite.

Fennel with Cream and Parmesan

Simple but delicious with a distinct Italian flavour! It's particularly good served with grilled fish or roast chicken. This method works well with celeriac too – cut into small dice or grated on the large holes of the grater.

Serves 4

3 or 4 fennel bulbs
1 tbsp olive oil
Freshly milled salt and black pepper
4–5 tbsp double cream
2–3 tbsp freshly grated Parmesan cheese

1. Trim the fennel and cut in half lengthways, keeping the base intact if possible. Cut each half, lengthways again, into four or five wedges.

2. Put the oil in a shallow pan and add the fennel. Cover and cook gently, turning occasionally, for about 10 minutes.

3. Add 2 tbsp water, cover and continue cooking for a further 10 minutes or until the fennel is tender and lightly browned.

4. Season with salt and pepper, stir in the cream and bubble gently for a minute or two.

5. Spoon the mixture into a shallow flameproof dish, making sure you scrape all the sauce from the pan. Sprinkle the Parmesan over the top.

6. Put under a hot grill until bubbling and golden brown.

To microwave:
1. Follow step 1 above.

2. Put the oil in a large casserole and stir in the fennel. Cover and cook on HIGH for 10 minutes, stirring occasionally.

3. Add 2 tbsp water, cover and cook on MEDIUM for 10 minutes or until the fennel is tender.

4. Season with salt and pepper, stir in the cream and bubble on HIGH for a minute or two.

5. As steps 5 and 6 above.

Chickpeas with Saffron and Spinach

Though this recipe was inspired by a Spanish dish made with similar ingredients, it also has a Middle Eastern feel about it. If time is really short, canned chickpeas could be used instead of dried. As well as a lovely side dish, it's suitable for serving as a main course with couscous. Or use a large spoonful as a bed on which to serve a fillet of pan-fried fish or grilled chicken.

Serves 4–6

**250g/9 oz dried chickpeas, soaked overnight in plenty of
   cold water**
2 tbsp olive oil
1 medium onion, thinly sliced into rings
1 garlic clove, finely chopped
Pinch of sugar
Pinch of saffron strands
½ tsp ground cumin
½ tsp ground coriander
400g can chopped tomatoes
Freshly milled salt and pepper
2 handfuls baby spinach leaves
Fresh lemon juice

1. Drain the chickpeas, put them into a large pan and cover with cold water. Bring to the boil and simmer gently for about 1 hour or until tender. (Do not add salt to the cooking water or the chickpeas may toughen.) Drain and reserve the cooking liquid.
2. Meanwhile, put the oil into a pan, add the onion and cook for 5–10 minutes, stirring occasionally, until soft but not browned.
3. Stir in the garlic, sugar, saffron, cumin and coriander. Cook, stirring, for a minute or two.
4. Add the drained chickpeas to the pan. Stir in the tomatoes and enough of the reserved cooking liquid to just cover.
5. Bring to the boil then simmer gently, uncovered, for about 30 minutes to allow the flavours to mingle and develop and the sauce to reduce a little. Season to taste.
6. Just before serving, remove from the heat and add the spinach leaves, stirring until just wilted. Add lemon juice to taste and serve immediately.

Tomato Gratin

Inspiration for this recipe came from a Provençale dish of stuffed tomatoes. Here the stuffing mixture is used as a topping for thickly sliced beefsteak tomatoes. Serve it as a snack with crusty bread or as a starter (cooked in individual serving dishes).

Serves 4

2 tbsp olive oil, plus extra for drizzling
4 beefsteak tomatoes, thickly sliced
85g/3 oz stale breadcrumbs
2 tbsp chopped fresh parsley
1 tbsp chopped fresh mint
1 garlic clove, finely chopped
1 tbsp capers, rinsed, drained and finely chopped
1 tsp dried oregano
Freshly milled salt and black pepper

1. Preheat the oven to 180°C, fan 160°C, 350°F, gas 4.

2. Lightly oil a shallow ovenproof dish and arrange the tomato slices, overlapping, in it.

3. Combine the breadcrumbs with the fresh herbs, garlic, capers, oregano and 2 tbsp oil. Season with salt and pepper.

4. Spoon the mixture over the tomatoes and drizzle with extra oil.

5. Put into the hot oven and cook for about 25 minutes until the tomatoes are soft but still intact and the topping is golden.

6. Serve immediately.

Pesto Sauce

This fresh-tasting Italian sauce has a multitude of uses. Stir it into freshly cooked pasta, spread it on toasted bread (crostini), spoon it alongside roasted vegetables, or dollop it on to a bowl of tomato or vegetable soup. Traditionally it is made with pine nuts and there is no reason why you should not use these instead of my choice of walnuts. You may also like to toast the nuts lightly first. Don't worry about measuring the ingredients too accurately – once the mixture is made, sample it and adjust the proportions to suit your own taste. Here are instructions for making it in a food processor; use a pestle in a large mortar if you prefer. Once made, keep it in a jar with a layer of olive oil on top.

Serves 4–6

50g/1¾ oz Parmesan cheese
1 small garlic clove, chopped
100g/3½ oz fresh basil leaves (about 3 handfuls)
70g/2½ oz walnuts (about 1 handful)
Freshly milled black pepper
About 200ml/7 fl oz extra virgin olive oil

1. Put the cheese and garlic into a food processor and pulse until finely chopped.

2. Add the basil leaves and pulse until chopped, scraping down the sides if necessary.

3. Add the walnuts and a few twists of black pepper and buzz briefly until roughly chopped.

4. With the motor running, add the oil in a thick stream.

Tomato Sauce

This is my basic tomato sauce for serving with pasta, fish, meat or vegetables. It may seem like a large amount but it freezes well. Unless you have a plentiful supply of sun-ripened, flavourful tomatoes, best results come from using a combination of fresh and canned. I don't bother to skin the fresh tomatoes (they hold a lot of flavour) – so long as you chop them up into small pieces and give the cooked sauce a quick buzz in the food processor, you won't notice. This recipe includes some red wine but you could use extra stock instead. Once the sauce is cooked and you are ready to serve, why not throw in some chopped fresh herbs, such as basil, thyme or parsley, or a chopped fresh chilli? To use the sauce on pizza (see page 41), simmer the puréed sauce, uncovered, gently until it reduces and thickens slightly.

Serves 8–12

2 tbsp olive oil
1 medium onion, finely chopped
1 celery stick, finely chopped
2 tsp sugar
2 garlic cloves, finely chopped or crushed
500g/1 lb 2 oz fresh ripe tomatoes, chopped into small
    pieces
400g çan tomatoes
300ml/½ pt red wine
300ml/½ pt chicken or vegetable stock
1 tbsp tomato purée
1 generous tsp freeze-dried oregano

1. Put the oil, onion, celery and sugar into a heavy-based pan and stir well. Cover and cook over medium heat for about 10 minutes, stirring occasionally, until softened but not browned.

2. Add the remaining ingredients and bring just to the boil. Cover and simmer gently for 15–20 minutes, stirring occasionally.

3. Remove the lid and continue simmering for a further 10 minutes.

4. Leave the sauce to cool slightly before tipping into a food processor and blending until the sauce is as chunky or as smooth as you want.

To microwave:

1. Put the oil, onion, celery and sugar into a large casserole and stir well. Cover and cook on HIGH for about 5 minutes or until soft, stirring once.

2. Stir in the remaining ingredients, cover and cook on HIGH for about 15 minutes, stirring occasionally.

3. Remove the cover and continue cooking on MEDIUM for about 10 minutes.

4. Continue as for step 4 opposite.

Green Herb Sauce

Store and serve this fresh sauce, called Salsa Verde, in the same way as pesto (see page 65). Again, don't be too particular about quantities; just remember to include equal amounts of the three herbs.

Serves 4–6

About 20g/¾ oz each of basil leaves, mint leaves and parsley
2 garlic cloves, finely chopped
2 tbsp capers, rinsed and drained
3 anchovy fillets
2 tsp Dijon mustard
Freshly milled black pepper
100–125ml/3½–4 fl oz olive oil

1. Put the herbs into a food processor and add the garlic, capers, anchovy fillets, mustard and a few twists of pepper. Buzz until fairly smooth, scraping down the sides if necessary.

2. With the motor running, add the oil in a thick stream.

Quick Tomato Sauce for Pizza

It is worth making double or triple quantities and storing it in pizza-size amounts in the fridge or freezer.

Tops about 2 large pizza bases (see page 41)

400g can plum tomatoes
1 tbsp olive oil
2 garlic cloves, thinly sliced
1 tbsp dried oregano
1 tsp sugar
Freshly milled salt and black pepper

1. Either put the tomatoes into a food processor and buzz until smooth or push them through a sieve (the latter method removes the seeds to give a smooth sauce).
2. Put the oil into a saucepan and add the tomatoes, garlic, oregano and sugar. Bring just to the boil then simmer gently for about 15 minutes, stirring more or less constantly to prevent the sauce spitting everywhere, or until thick. Season to taste with salt and pepper.

Rouille

Rouille is French for 'rust coloured', which is an excellent description of this fiery sauce that originates in Provence. It is delicious served as a garnish with fish soups and stews, stirred in just before serving.

Makes about 150ml/¼ pt

2 large garlic cloves
½ small red pepper, seeds removed and chopped
1–2 red chillies, seeds removed and chopped
Pinch of saffron strands
1 slice of bread, crusts removed
5 tbsp olive oil
Fish stock or water

1. Using a pestle and mortar, pound the garlic, pepper, chillies and saffron to a paste.
2. Soak the bread in a little fish stock or water and squeeze dry.
3. Pound the bread with the chilli mixture until smooth.
4. Add the oil drop by drop, stirring with the pestle all the while, until the sauce is thick and creamy.

Mayonnaise

This sharp-tasting mayonnaise is made in a food processor or blender – nothing could be easier. For best results, make sure all the ingredients are at room temperature. Before you start, put the kettle on because you may need a little boiling water at the end. I use a mixture of oils, though you may prefer the distinctive flavour of mayonnaise made entirely with olive oil. Either way, store it in the fridge and use within 3–4 days.

Makes about 300ml/½ pt

1 medium egg
1 medium egg yolk
½ tsp ready-made mustard
¼ tsp salt
2 tbsp lemon juice or wine vinegar
Freshly milled white pepper
150ml/¼ pt olive oil
150ml/¼ pt sunflower oil

1.   Put the egg and egg yolk into a food processor or blender and add the mustard, salt, half the lemon juice and a twist of pepper. Buzz until smooth.

2.   Put the oils into a jug and with the machine running, drizzle them into the egg mixture in a thin stream. As soon as the sauce thickens add the remaining lemon juice (with the processor running all the time) then slowly add the remaining oil. If the sauce is too thick, blend in 1 tbsp boiling water.

3.   Transfer to a bowl, cover and chill until required.

Aioli

Serve this garlicky mayonnaise from the Provence region of France with sticks of raw vegetables (crudités) for dipping, with grilled fish (tuna in particular) or meat, or with fish soup.

Makes about 425ml/¾ pt

6–8 garlic cloves
2 medium egg yolks
Juice of 1 lemon
Freshly milled salt and pepper
425ml/¾ pt olive oil

1. Put the garlic, egg yolks, lemon juice and seasoning into the blender and blend on medium speed until smooth.

2. Pour the oil into a jug and, with the machine running, slowly pour into the blender in a thin stream until thick.

3. Cover and chill until required.

Anchoiade

Spread this anchovy paste on bread or toast, or stir it into fish or tomato soup (as you would rouille, page 68). It's also good served with hard-boiled eggs, fish, steaks and jacket potatoes.

Serves 4–6

50g can anchovies in olive oil
2 garlic cloves, chopped
1 egg yolk
1 tbsp wine vinegar (white or red)
150ml/¼ pt olive oil

1. Drain the anchovies, reserving the oil, and chop.

2. Put the chopped anchovies into a food processor or blender. Add the garlic, egg yolk and vinegar. Buzz until smooth, scraping down the sides if necessary.

3. With the motor running, drizzle in the olive and anchovy oils until the mixture thickens like mayonnaise.

4. Spoon into a bowl, cover and chill until required.

Sauces for Pasta

These simple-but-delicious sauces for stirring into hot drained pasta take minutes to make. Each sauce serves 2. Try other recipes in this book too, such as tomato sauce on page 66, pesto sauce on page 65, olive paste on page 26 and Salsa Verde on page 67.

Anchovy Sauce

Drain a 50g can of anchovies (reserving the oil) and chop them finely. Combine them with 3 tbsp chopped flat-leaf parsley, some freshly milled black pepper and a squeeze of lemon juice. Stir in the reserved anchovy oil.

Black Olive, Sundried Tomato and Caper Sauce

Chop 50g/1¾ oz pitted black olives and about 6 sundried tomatoes. Combine them with 1 tbsp capers, 1 tbsp chopped fresh herbs (thyme or oregano are good) and 3–4 tbsp olive oil.

Tuna, Lemon and Chilli

Heat 2 tbsp olive oil and stir in a pinch of chilli flakes. Add the finely grated rind and juice of half a lemon, about 3 tbsp chopped fresh herbs (parsley, mint, coriander) and a drained and flaked 20g can tuna. Heat through gently and season to taste.

Melting Cheese Sauce

Dice about 175g/6 oz goat's cheese or blue cheese (such as Gorgonzola) with 2–3 tbsp olive oil and some freshly milled black pepper.

Creamy Mushroom and Parmesan

Cook about 225g/8 oz thickly sliced button mushrooms in 2 tbsp olive oil until golden brown. Add 1 finely chopped garlic clove, 4 tbsp dry white wine or vermouth, 4 tbsp double cream and seasoning. Bubble gently for a few minutes then stir in grated Parmesan cheese to taste and a little chopped parsley.

4

MAIN MEALS

With good quality ingredients and simple cooking it is possible to bring the flavours of the Mediterranean to your table at any time of the year. After all, what can be more delicious than a choice piece of fish, chicken, lamb or pork, first rubbed with olive oil and seasoned with herbs such as thyme and oregano, then cooked under a hot grill or on a ridged griddle pan? Or how about a platter of roasted vegetables, or some grilled kebabs threaded with seasoned chicken, or a whole fish baked in the oven with orange and lemon slices and plenty of fresh herbs?

Take advantage of the wide range of fresh, filled pasta that is on offer today. Choose your favourite shape and filling, cook it and pour over some olive oil that has been gently heated with some chopped fresh leaves of sage or thyme. Or think of tossing some couscous or pasta shapes with strips of grilled red and yellow peppers and serving with a fresh tomato sauce (page 66).

As you cook your way through this chapter, expect to experience some wonderful scents and complex flavours. From moussaka to souvlaki, gnocchi to risotto, tagine to tortilla and couscous to pilaf, there is something here for everyone.

Tortilla

Tortilla is the Spanish name for this round, open omelette, which makes a regular appearance in tapas bars. In Italy it is known as Fritatta. Here is a fairly plain though delicious recipe, to which you could add various ingredients: garlic, chilli, herbs, olives, chorizo, pancetta, mushrooms, seasonal vegetables and even small cubes of cheese – the choice is yours. Served cold in wedges, tortilla makes a great addition to a packed lunch, a picnic or any meal outdoors.

Serves 4–6

2 tbsp olive oil
1 medium onion, thinly sliced
2 medium potatoes, cut into small dice
1 small red pepper, seeds removed and thinly sliced
5 eggs
Freshly milled salt and pepper

1. Put half the oil into a large (preferably non-stick) frying pan and add the onion, potatoes and red pepper. Cover and cook over medium heat for about 10 minutes, stirring occasionally, until the potatoes are tender and the whole mixture is just beginning to turn golden brown.

2. In a large jug or bowl, beat the eggs and season with salt and pepper. Stir the vegetable mixture into the eggs.

3. Wipe the pan out and add the remaining oil. When hot, add the egg-and-vegetable mixture, spreading it evenly over the base of the pan.

4. Cook gently over medium-to-low heat, without stirring, until the egg has set on the base and around the edge of the pan (the top surface will remain uncooked).

5. Sliding a spatula around the edges to loosen the omelette, carefully slide it on to a flat plate. Now invert the pan over the plate and use it to flip the omelette over. Continue cooking for a minute or two until the bottom (which was the top) has set.

6. Cut into wedges and serve.

Minestrone

Minestrone is Italian for 'big soup'. It usually refers to a soup that is thick with vegetables and includes pasta and sometimes beans or peas. As a starter only a small serving is needed; make it into a complete meal by topping large bowlfuls with freshly grated Parmesan cheese and/or swirling in a spoonful of home-made pesto (page 65).

Serves 4

1 tbsp olive oil
2 bacon rashers, finely chopped (optional)
1 small onion, finely chopped
1 garlic clove, finely chopped
2 medium carrots, cut into small dice
2 celery sticks, thinly sliced
850ml/1½ pt vegetable stock
3 sun-dried tomatoes, finely chopped
400g can haricot beans, drained
50g/1¾ oz small pasta shapes
75g/2¾ oz cabbage, finely shredded
2 tbsp chopped fresh parsley
Freshly milled salt and black pepper

1. Put the oil and bacon into a pan and cook, stirring occasionally, until just beginning to turn golden brown.

2. Add the onion, garlic, carrots and celery and continue cooking for about 5 minutes, stirring occasionally.

3. Add the stock and bring to the boil. Cover and simmer gently for about 10 minutes.

4. Stir in the tomatoes, beans and pasta. Simmer gently for 8–10 minutes, stirring once or twice, until the pasta is just tender.

5. Stir in the cabbage and parsley, remove from the heat, season to taste and leave to stand for 2–3 minutes.

To microwave:

1.   Put the oil and bacon into a large casserole, cover and microwave on HIGH for 2–3 minutes, stirring once.

2.   Add the onion, garlic, carrots and celery. Stir in half the stock (which should be hot). Cover and microwave on HIGH for about 5 minutes, stirring once or twice, until the vegetables are just tender.

3.   Stir in the tomatoes, beans, pasta and remaining (hot) stock. Microwave on HIGH for about 5 minutes, stirring occasionally, or until the soup comes to the boil and the pasta is just tender.

4.   Stir in the cabbage and parsley. Cook on HIGH for 2–3 minutes. Season to taste.

Pissaladière

*A Niçoise onion tart – make it with a pizza base as in this recipe
or with shortcrust pastry. If you have a food processor or a
mandolin, make life easy and use the slicing disc to cut the
onions. Though the rosemary sprig is optional, its inclusion
makes a marked difference to the flavour of the onions. You
could use the oil from the anchovies in place of olive oil too.
Serve it warm or at room temperature with a green and/or a
tomato salad.*

Serves 4–6

3 tbsp olive oil
1kg/1¼ lb onions, thinly sliced
1 generous tsp dried thyme or 1 tbsp fresh thyme leaves
1 sprig of fresh rosemary (optional)
1 tsp sugar
Freshly milled salt and black pepper (optional)
Half quantity of pizza dough (see page 41)
115g can anchovy fillets in oil, drained and halved
    lengthways
Black olives

1. Put the oil in a large, preferably non-stick, pan and add the
    onions, herbs and sugar. Cover and cook gently, stirring
    occasionally, until the onions are very soft but not coloured
    (this may take a good 20 minutes).

2. Remove the lid, turn up the heat and continue cooking the
    onion mixture, stirring frequently, until it is a rich golden
    brown. Taste and season lightly with salt and pepper if
    required.

3. Put a large flat baking sheet in the oven and preheat to
    200°C, fan 180°C, 400°F, gas 6.

4. Meanwhile, roll out the pizza dough to fit a second baking
    sheet (about 30cm/12 in square).

5. Spread the onion mixture over the dough, almost to the
    edges. Arrange the anchovy pieces in a criss-cross pattern
    over the top and drop an olive into each square.

6. Put the baking sheet on to the preheated one in the oven
    and cook for 15–20 minutes until golden brown and
    cooked through.

Spinach and Cheese Pie

In Greece this wonderful dish is called Spanakopita or, when the spinach and cheese mixture is used to fill small triangular pastry parcels, Tyropittakia. I tend to use frozen leaf spinach though you can of course use fresh leaves – just cook them lightly, drain and squeeze out the liquid as below. If you like, replace some of the feta cheese (which can be quite salty) with coarsely grated Cheddar or mozzarella. Try adding some toasted pine nuts to the filling too. Filo pastry can dry out quickly, so keep the unused sheets covered while you work.

Makes a 23cm/9 in square pie

1 tbsp olive oil
2 medium onions, finely chopped
½ tsp freshly grated nutmeg
500g/1 lb 2 oz frozen leaf spinach, thawed
400g/14 oz feta cheese, finely chopped or crumbled
2 large eggs, lightly beaten
Freshly milled black pepper
Melted butter
10 large sheets of filo pastry

1. Put the oil and onions into a pan and cook over medium heat for 5–10 minutes, stirring occasionally, until very soft and just beginning to turn golden brown. Stir in the nutmeg and remove from the heat.
2. Using your hand, squeeze the excess liquid from the spinach then chop it roughly. Stir into the onions.
3. Combine the spinach mixture with the cheese, eggs and seasoning.
4. Preheat the oven to 180°C, fan 160°C, 350°F, gas 4.
5. Brush the inside of a 23cm/9 in square cake tin with melted butter. Line the tin with a pastry sheet, gently pushing it into the corners and allowing the excess to hang over the sides. Brush the pastry lightly with butter. Turn the tin 90 degrees and add a second layer of pastry, brushing it with a little butter. Repeat with two or three more sheets.
6. Spoon the filling into the pastry case, levelling the top.
7. Cover with four or five layers of pastry, brushing each one with butter. Trim the edges.
8. Put into the hot oven and cook for about 45 minutes until crisp and golden brown.
9. Leave to cool slightly before cutting into squares. Serve warm or at room temperature.

Spiced Chickpeas

The addition of harissa, saffron and cinnamon gives this dish a distinct Middle Eastern flavour. If you are in a hurry, use drained, canned chickpeas instead of dried. Serve spooned over couscous, bulgur wheat or rice.

Serves 4

250g/9 oz dried chickpeas, soaked overnight in plenty of cold water
2 tbsp olive oil
1 medium onion, finely chopped
1 medium carrot, finely chopped
2.5cm/1 in piece root ginger, grated
400ml/14 fl oz vegetable stock
½ tsp ground cinnamon
Pinch of saffron strands
2 tbsp tomato purée
1–2 tsp harissa paste, to suit your taste
2 ripe tomatoes
Freshly milled salt and black pepper
Handful of roughly chopped coriander

1. Drain the chickpeas, put them into a large saucepan and cover with cold water. Bring to the boil then simmer for about 1 hour or until tender.

2. Put the oil, onion, carrot and ginger into a large pan and cook over medium heat for 5–10 minutes, stirring occasionally, until soft but not browned.

3. Drain the chickpeas and add to the pan. Stir in the stock, cinnamon, saffron, tomato purée and harissa. Bring to the boil then lower the heat and simmer gently for about 30 minutes.

4. Meanwhile, put the tomatoes in a bowl and pour over boiling water to cover them. Leave to stand for a minute or two before draining and the skins should slip off easily. Discard the skins and chop the tomatoes finely.

5. Just before serving, adjust the seasoning to taste and stir in the tomatoes and coriander.

Couscous with Apricots, Feta and Pine Nuts

The feta cheese is added just before serving and allowed to soften only slightly. Toast the pine nuts until golden brown in a dry frying pan on the hob, under a medium-hot grill or in a hot oven.

Serves 4

2 tbsp olive oil, plus extra for drizzling
2 medium onions, thinly sliced
1 garlic clove, finely chopped
1 tsp ground mixed spice
600ml/1 pt vegetable stock
115g/4 oz ready-to-eat dried apricots, chopped
Freshly milled black pepper
250g/9 oz couscous
200g feta cheese, cut into small cubes
3–4 tbsp pine nuts, toasted (see above)
2 tbsp chopped fresh parsley

1. Put the oil and onions into a large pan and cook for 10–15 minutes, stirring occasionally, until soft and golden brown.

2. Stir in the garlic and mixed spice and cook, stirring, for 1–2 minutes.

3. Add the stock, apricots and black pepper. Bring to the boil, cover and simmer gently for 5–10 minutes.

4. Stir in the couscous, remove from the heat, cover and leave to stand for a further 5–10 minutes until all the liquid has been absorbed and the couscous is tender.

5. Gently stir in the feta cheese, pine nuts and parsley. Cover and leave to stand for a few minutes before serving (drizzled with a little extra olive oil if wished).

Mushroom Risotto

The traditional way to make a risotto is to stir it lovingly, adding the stock little by little until the rice is cooked yet still retains a slight bite and the small amount of sauce pooling around it is creamy. For those who might not want to stand at the cooker for the entire time, I have given the method for oven cooking at the end of the recipe. Incidentally, the rosemary sprig imparts a wonderfully subtle flavour to the rice before it is discarded prior to serving.

Serves 4

15g dried wild porcini mushrooms
600ml/1 pt light vegetable or chicken stock or mixture of
   the two
2 tbsp olive oil
1 medium onion, finely chopped
1 garlic clove, finely chopped
250g/9 oz risotto rice, such as carnaroli or arborio
175g/6 oz mushrooms, such as chestnut, chopped or
   sliced
Sprig of fresh rosemary
150ml/¼ pt dry white wine
Freshly milled salt and black pepper
3 tbsp freshly grated Parmesan cheese
25g/1 oz butter, cut into small cubes
2 tbsp finely chopped parsley
Flakes of Parmesan cheese, to serve

1.   Put the dried mushrooms into a bowl, pour 300ml/½ pt boiling water over them and leave to stand for 20 minutes. Lift out the mushrooms and chop them finely.

2.   Put the soaking liquid from the mushrooms into a saucepan, making sure that you don't add any grit which may have settled at the bottom. Add the stock and bring the mixture to the gentlest simmer.

3.   Put the oil, onion and garlic into a large heavy-based pan and cook over medium heat for 5–10 minutes, stirring frequently, until soft but not browned.

4.   Add the rice and cook, stirring, for about 2 minutes. Stir in the fresh mushrooms and add the rosemary sprig.

5. Add the wine and cook, stirring, until it has been absorbed.

6. Stirring all the time, add the hot stock a ladleful at a time, waiting until the liquid has been absorbed before the next addition, until the rice is cooked. This will take about 20 minutes.

7. Season with pepper (and salt only if absolutely necessary). Stir in the grated Parmesan, the butter and parsley.

8. Serve in warmed shallow bowls topped with Parmesan flakes.

To cook the risotto in the oven:
Use a heavy-based ovenproof pan or casserole and complete steps 1–5. Stir in all the stock mixture, bring to the boil and put into a preheated oven at 150°C, fan 130°C, 300°F, gas 2. Cook uncovered for 25 minutes then complete steps 7 and 8.

Gnocchi with Tomatoes and Taleggio

Gnocchi are small Italian dumplings usually made from potatoes, flour and eggs. In some parts of Italy they may be made with semolina. The simplest way of serving them is with butter and freshly grated Parmesan cheese. Here, they are served in a fresh-tasting sauce of tomatoes and topped with creamy cheese. Taleggio is my preferred choice but chèvre (goat's cheese) or mozzarella are good too. Hand round some crusty bread to mop up the juices.

Serves 4

500g/1 lb 2 oz fresh ripe tomatoes
25g/1 oz butter
½ tsp sugar
Freshly milled salt and black pepper
Handful of fresh basil leaves
Two 400g packs gnocchi
150–200g/5½-7 oz Taleggio cheese, thinly sliced

1. Put the tomatoes in a bowl and pour over boiling water to cover them. Leave to stand for a minute or two before draining and the skins should slip off easily. Discard the skins and chop the tomatoes finely.

2. Melt the butter in a pan and add the tomatoes, sugar and seasoning. Heat until bubbling then stir in the basil. Remove from the heat.

3. Cook the gnocchi following packet instructions and drain.

4. Stir the drained gnocchi into the tomatoes and tip the mixture into a flameproof dish.

5. Top with the cheese and put under a hot grill until bubbling and golden.

6. Serve immediately.

Aubergines with Tomatoes and Cheese

My version of the Italian dish known as Aubergine Parmigiana.
Serve it with some crusty bread.

Serves 4–6

500ml carton passata (sieved tomatoes)
2 garlic cloves, finely chopped
Handful of fresh basil leaves, chopped
Freshly milled salt and black pepper
1kg/2¼ lb aubergines, thinly sliced lengthways
Olive oil
400g/14 oz mozzarella cheese, grated
50g/1¾ oz freshly grated Parmesan cheese

1. Mix together the passata, garlic and basil. Season with salt and pepper.

2. Brush the aubergine slices lightly with olive oil. Heat a large griddle or non-stick frying pan and cook the aubergines on both sides until soft and browned. (Alternatively brown them under a hot grill.)

3. Preheat the oven to 180°C, fan 160°C, 350°F, gas 4.

4. Arrange one-third of the aubergine slices in a shallow ovenproof dish and spread with one-third of the tomato sauce. Scatter with one third of the mozzarella and Parmesan cheeses. Repeat this process twice more.

5. Put into the hot oven and cook for about 30 minutes until bubbling hot and golden brown on top.

6. Leave to stand for 5–10 minutes to settle before cutting and serving.

Fish in Parcels

The fish listed here make up a selection of Mediterranean varieties but you could always use salmon, cod, haddock and the like. This really is a 'make-it-up-as-you-go' recipe, where you could use herbs in season plus black or green olives or capers in place of the nuts – be creative! Let everyone open their own parcels and I wager they will all say 'Mmmmm'.

Serves as many as you make

For each parcel:
Olive oil
1 fish fillet weighing about 175g/6 oz, such as tuna, red mullet, monkfish, bream or bass
Small sprig of herb, such as rosemary, thyme, oregano, fennel or parsley
About 2 tsp chopped pistachio nuts
About 4 cherry tomatoes, halved
Freshly milled salt and pepper
Finely grated lemon rind
Fresh lemon juice

1. Put one or more flat baking sheets into the oven and preheat to 180°C, fan 160°C, 350°F, gas 4.

2. Cut a large piece of thick foil and brush one side with a little olive oil. Lay the fish fillet on it and top with the herb, nuts, tomatoes and seasoning. Add a good pinch of lemon rind, a squeeze of lemon juice and a drizzle of olive oil.

3. Fold the foil up loosely and crimp the edges, sealing them to make a parcel.

4. Put the parcel(s) on the baking sheet(s) in the hot oven and cook for 20 minutes.

Mussels in White Wine with Cream

My version of Moules à la Marinière with the addition of garlic and a little cream. Serve it in large shallow bowls with fresh crusty bread to mop up the soup-like sauce.

Serves 4 as a starter, 2 as a main course

1kg/2¼ lb mussels in their shells
2 tbsp olive oil
3 shallots, finely chopped
1 garlic clove, finely chopped
Freshly milled black pepper
150ml/¼ pt dry white wine
2 tbsp double cream
2 tbsp chopped fresh parsley

1. Scrub the mussels, scraping off any barnacles and discarding any with broken shells or that do not close when given a (really) sharp tap. Pull off the stringy beards with a sharp tug.

2. Put the oil, shallots and garlic into a very large pan and cook over medium heat for about 5 minutes, stirring frequently, until very soft but not browned. Season with pepper.

3. Add the wine and immediately tip in the mussels. Cover with a lid and cook quickly, shaking the pan occasionally, for 4–5 minutes or until the mussels have just opened (do not be tempted to overcook them).

4. Remove the lid, stir in the cream and parsley and bubble gently for a minute or two.

5. Serve immediately.

Paella

This Spanish dish is traditionally made and served in a large, flat, two-handled pan called a paella pan.

Serves 4

4 tbsp olive oil
1 onion, finely chopped
2 garlic cloves, finely chopped
4 boneless chicken thighs, skin removed and each one cut
   into about 4 pieces
1 red pepper, seeds removed and chopped
1 green pepper, seeds removed and chopped
2 tomatoes, seeds removed and chopped
400g/14 oz paella rice or risotto rice
50g/1¾ oz chorizo or spicy sausage, sliced or chopped
1 litre/1¾ pt chicken stock
Freshly milled black pepper
Pinch of saffron strands
About 300g/10½ oz skinless white fish, such as cod, cut
   into bite-size pieces
About 12 mussels, scrubbed and stringy beards removed
About 12 raw tiger prawns in their shells

1. Put the oil, onion and garlic into a paella pan or a wide frying pan and cook gently for 5–10 minutes, stirring occasionally, until softened but not browned.

2. Add the chicken, increase the heat and cook for a few minutes until lightly browned.

3. Stir in the peppers and tomatoes.

4. Add the rice and cook, stirring for a minute or two until the rice grains are well coated with oil

5. Stir in the chorizo, stock, black pepper and saffron and bring just to the boil. Reduce the heat and simmer gently (uncovered and preferably without stirring) for about 20 minutes or until the rice is just cooked.

6. Add the fish, mussels and prawns and continue cooking for about 5 minutes, stirring gently, or until just cooked through.

7. Serve immediately.

Spinach and Ricotta Cannelloni

Various fillings can be used to make this Italian-style dish. Though I prefer to use sheets of lasagne rolled around the stuffing, you could of course use large pasta tubes. Spinach and ricotta cheese make a lovely light filling.

Serves 4

500g/1 lb 2 oz fresh spinach leaves
8 fresh lasagne sheets
250g ricotta cheese
60g/2¼ oz freshly grated Parmesan, plus extra for topping
Good pinch of freshly grated nutmeg
Freshly milled salt and black pepper
600ml/1 pt milk
25g/1 oz plain flour
40g/1½ oz butter

1. Cook the spinach until just wilted (either in the microwave or in a pan of hot water on the hob). Drain well and squeeze out any excess liquid before chopping finely.

2. Drop the lasagne sheets into boiling water for a minute or two until soft. Drain and dry on kitchen paper.

3. Mix the spinach with the ricotta and Parmesan cheeses, nutmeg and seasoning to taste.

4. Place a spoonful of the spinach mixture on to each pasta sheet and roll up. Arrange the rolls in a shallow buttered ovenproof dish so that they are almost touching in a single layer.

5. Preheat the oven to 190°C, fan 170°C, 375°F, gas 5.

6. Put the milk, flour and butter into a saucepan and whisk until combined. Bring to the boil, stirring with the whisk, until thickened.

7. Pour the sauce over the cannelloni, making sure that all the pasta is covered. Sprinkle with extra Parmesan cheese.

8. Put into the hot oven and cook for about 25 minutes until bubbling and golden brown.

Moussaka

Though this aromatic Greek dish takes time to make, it's well worth the effort. Make it with lamb or beef or a mixture of the two. Adding breadcrumbs to the topping is an option if you want a little extra crunch.

Serves 6

About 1 kg/2¼ lb aubergines, trimmed and cut lengthways into 5mm/¼ in slices
Olive oil
1 large onion, finely chopped
1 large garlic clove, finely chopped
½ tsp ground cinnamon
½ tsp ground allspice
500g/1 lb 2 oz lean lamb mince
100ml/3½ fl oz red wine
400g can chopped tomatoes
1 rounded tsp dried oregano
Freshly milled salt and pepper
600ml/1 pt milk
50g/1¾ oz plain flour
50g/1¾ oz butter, cut into small pieces
2 eggs, beaten
50g/1¾ oz freshly grated Parmesan cheese
3 tbsp fresh breadcrumbs (optional)

1. Brush the aubergine slices lightly with olive oil. Heat a large griddle or non-stick frying pan and cook the aubergines on both sides until soft and browned. (Alternatively brown them under a hot grill.)

2. Make the meat sauce. Put 1 tbsp olive oil into a large saucepan, add the onion and cook over medium heat for 5–10 minutes, stirring occasionally until soft but not browned. Stir in the garlic, cinnamon and allspice. Crumble in the mince and cook, stirring occasionally, until the lamb is no longer pink. Add the wine, tomatoes, oregano and seasoning. Bring just to the boil then cover and simmer gently for about 30 minutes (remove the lid for the final 10 minutes so that the sauce thickens slightly).

3. Make the white sauce. Put the milk, flour and butter into a saucepan and whisk well. Cook, whisking gently, until the sauce comes to the boil and thickens. Allow it to bubble for a minute or two. Season to taste with salt and pepper.

Remove the pan from the heat and stir in the eggs and half the Parmesan cheese.

4. Preheat the oven to 190°C, fan 170°C, 375°F, gas 5.

5. In a shallow ovenproof dish, put a layer of aubergine (about one third of the slices). Spread half the meat sauce over the top. Add a second layer of aubergine followed by the remaining meat sauce. Finish with the remaining aubergine. Spoon the white sauce over the top and sprinkle with the breadcrumbs (if using) and the remaining Parmesan cheese.

6. Put into the hot oven and cook for about 40 minutes until bubbling hot throughout and golden brown on top.

7. Leave to stand for 5–10 minutes to settle before cutting and serving.

Spaghetti with Clams and Tomatoes

In Italy, this would be Spaghetti alle Vongole. It's equally good made with mussels or mixed seafood. In the absence of fresh, I have been known to use drained jars of clams. Serve it in large shallow bowls as a substantial main course or in smaller portions as the first course of a special meal.

Serves 4

675g/1½ lb fresh clams
350g/12 oz dried spaghetti
3 tbsp olive oil
1 small onion, finely chopped
1 garlic clove, finely chopped
1 small red chilli, seeds removed and finely chopped
100ml/3½ fl oz dry white wine
400g can chopped tomatoes
2 tbsp chopped fresh parsley

1. Scrub the clams and discard any with broken shells or that do not close when given a sharp tap.

2. Put the pasta on to boil, following packet instructions.

3. Meanwhile, put the oil in a large pan, add the onion and cook over medium heat for about 5 minutes, stirring occasionally, until softened but not browned. Stir in the garlic and chilli and cook for 1–2 minutes. Add the wine and bring to the boil, then stir in the tomatoes. Simmer gently for 5 minutes, stirring frequently.

4. Add the clams and parsley to the tomato mixture, stirring well. Cover and cook for about 2 minutes or until the shells have opened (discard any that remain unopened).

5. Drain the spaghetti and toss with the clams and their sauce.

6. Serve immediately.

Lamb Keftethes

Greek Keftethes, or Kephtedes, are made with minced meat, fish or vegetables and usually shaped on to skewers or into small balls. They can be fried, grilled or barbecued and served as part of a mezze (appetiser or first course) or as a main dish. Try serving them in warmed and split pitta bread with some shredded crisp lettuce, sliced cucumber and a spoonful of Greek yogurt (with some finely chopped mint and freshly milled pepper stirred into it). They are quite delicious cold too.

Serves 4–5

1 large onion, roughly chopped
2 garlic cloves
2 medium slices of bread (about 75g/2½ oz in total)
A small handful of fresh mint leaves
A few sprigs of fresh parsley
1 tsp ground cumin
500g/1 lb 2 oz lean minced lamb
1 medium egg
Freshly milled salt and black pepper
Olive oil

1. Put the onion, garlic and bread into a food processor and blend until finely chopped. Add the herbs, cumin, lamb, egg and seasoning and blend until well mixed.

2. Using your hands, either shape the mixture along four or five flat metal skewers (like a sausage about 15–20cm/6–8 inches long) or make about 20 small balls.

3. Cover and refrigerate for 1–2 hours or until needed.

4. To cook the skewers, brush with a little oil and cook (under a grill or on the barbecue) on medium-to-high heat for about 8–10 minutes, turning occasionally, until cooked through. To cook meatballs, heat some oil in a frying pan, add the meatballs (in a single layer and with plenty of space between them), turning them until golden brown all over and cooked through.

5. To serve, carefully slide the cooked lamb off the skewers or drain the meatballs. Serve immediately.

Spiced Lamb with Preserved Lemon

A Moroccan-style stew or tagine (see also Chicken with Olives and Preserved Lemon on page 102). Serve it with freshly cooked couscous, bulgur wheat or rice.

Serves 4–6

3 tbsp olive oil
1kg/2¼ lb lean lamb (such as shoulder), cut into large
  cubes
2 tsp ras el hanout (see page 19)
1 tsp ground cumin
1 tsp ground cinnamon
1 tsp ground ginger
1 tsp paprika
3 medium onions, sliced
2 garlic cloves, finely chopped
400g can chopped tomatoes
3 medium carrots, thickly sliced
150ml/¼ pt red wine, stock or water
2 preserved lemons, seeds removed, thinly sliced
Chopped fresh coriander

1. Heat the oil in a large ovenproof casserole and quickly brown the lamb.

2. Add the spices and cook, stirring, for 1–2 minutes.

3. Stir in the onions, garlic, tomatoes, carrots and red wine. Bring just to the boil.

4. Cover and cook in the oven at 170°C, fan 150°C, 325°F, gas 3 for about 1 hour.

5. Add the preserved lemons and continue cooking for a further 30 minutes or until the lamb is very tender.

6. Stir in some coriander and serve.

Lamb Kleftiko

In this Greek dish, lamb is cooked in a parcel with garlic, lemon, herbs (oregano in particular) and olive oil until it is meltingly tender. Everyone gets to open his or her own parcel and appreciate the aromatic whiffs that waft out. You could of course use a large ovenproof casserole with a light-fitting lid instead.

Serves 4

4 tbsp olive oil
2 medium-to-large potatoes, scrubbed and cut into wedges
1 large carrot, thinly sliced
Freshly milled salt and pepper
4 leg steaks of lamb or lean chops
2 garlic cloves, thinly sliced
4 sprigs of fresh oregano or 2 tsp dried
A few fresh mint leaves or ½ tsp dried
Juice of 1 lemon

1. Preheat the oven to 180°C, fan 160°C, 350°F, gas 4.

2. Cut four large squares of thick foil.

3. Onto each square, drizzle a little of the olive oil. Add the potatoes and carrot, seasoning them with salt and pepper. Lay the lamb on top and sprinkle with the garlic, herbs and lemon juice. Drizzle over the remaining oil.

4. Gather up the foil loosely and seal the edges well to make four parcels. Put them on a large baking sheet with a little space between each.

5. Put into the hot oven and cook for about 1 hour.

Lasagne

Sheets of pasta are layered with a meat sauce that is delicately flavoured with fennel seeds and topped with white sauce and cheese. The addition of a small amount of chopped chicken livers might make the recipe more authentic (depending on the region of Italy you visit). Some sliced mozzarella cheese could be added to the layers too if you like.

Serves 6

1 tbsp olive oil
5 unsmoked bacon rashers, rinds removed and finely
   chopped
1 large onion, finely chopped
3 medium carrots, finely chopped
4 celery sticks, finely chopped
2 garlic cloves, finely chopped
800g/1¾ lb lean minced beef, or a mixture of beef and pork
100ml/3½ fl oz dry white wine or vermouth
4 tbsp tomato purée
2 tsp fennel seeds
300ml/½ pt beef or vegetable stock
500ml/18 fl oz milk
3 tbsp plain flour
40g/1½ oz butter
Freshly milled salt and pepper
60g/2¼ oz freshly grated Parmesan cheese
About 12 sheets of fresh or dried lasagne

1. To make the meat sauce, put the oil and bacon into a large saucepan and cook over medium heat, stirring occasionally, until the bacon just starts to turn golden brown. Add the onion, carrots, celery and garlic and cook for 5–10 minutes, stirring occasionally, until the vegetables have softened slightly but not browned. Add the mince and cook quickly until no longer pink, stirring well to break it up. Stir in the wine, then the tomato purée, fennel seeds and stock. Bring to the boil then simmer gently for about 15 minutes.

2. Meanwhile make the white sauce. Put the milk into a saucepan and add the flour and butter. Stirring continuously with a whisk, heat until the mixture comes to the boil and thickens. Season to taste with salt and pepper.

3. Preheat the oven to 190°C, fan 170°C, 375°F, gas 5.

4. In a shallow ovenproof dish spread one-third of the meat sauce, drizzle with a couple of tablespoonfuls of white sauce and sprinkle a little Parmesan over. Arrange 4 lasagne sheets on the top. Repeat the layers twice more. Spoon the remaining white sauce over the top, making sure that the pasta is completely covered and scatter the remaining Parmesan over the surface.

5. Put into the hot oven and cook for about 40 minutes until soft throughout and the top is golden brown.

6. To make cutting easier, leave the lasagne to stand and settle for 5–10 minutes before serving hot.

Pork Souvlaki

These simple herb-coated Greek kebabs are traditionally made with pieces of meat, fish or vegetables threaded on to skewers. Serve them with a salad of watercress and sliced ripe tomatoes together with some lemon wedges for squeezing over. Alternatively, serve them in warmed and split pitta bread.

Serves 6

4 tbsp olive oil
2 garlic cloves, crushed
1 tbsp wine vinegar or fresh lemon juice
3 tbsp mixed dried herbs (equal quantities of oregano, thyme and marjoram work well)
Freshly milled salt and black pepper
About 800g/1¾ lb lean pork, cut into cubes

1. Put all the ingredients except the pork into a large bowl and whisk well. Add the pork and toss well until coated. Cover and leave to marinate in the refrigerator for about 2 hours, stirring occasionally if convenient.

2. Thread the pork on to flat metal skewers and brush with any remaining marinade.

3. Put under a medium-hot grill (or on the barbecue) and cook for about 20 minutes, turning occasionally and brushing with any extra marinade, until cooked through.

Meatballs Italian Style

Meatballs or patties are to be found all over the Mediterranean. Turn to page 91 and you will find a Greek variety (Keftethes) made with lamb. Try the version below served on a mound of freshly cooked spaghetti or tagliatelle with a spoonful or two of Tomato Sauce (page 66) and topped with a little freshly grated Parmesan cheese. They also make a delicious appetiser when made into tiny balls and served warm or at room temperature on cocktail sticks, with or without a dip.

Makes 20–25

1 large onion, roughly chopped
75g/2¾ oz fresh bread, cut into pieces
1 tsp dried thyme
¼ tsp freshly grated nutmeg
2–3 tbsp chopped fresh parsley
1 egg
500g/1 lb 2 oz lean ground minced beef, pork or turkey
4 tbsp freshly grated Parmesan cheese, or mature Cheddar
Freshly milled salt and black pepper
Olive oil for frying

1. Put the onion and bread into a food processor and add the thyme, nutmeg and parsley. Blend until finely chopped. Add the egg, meat, cheese and seasoning and blend until well mixed, breaking up the meat and scraping down the sides if necessary.

2. Using your hands, shape the mixture into balls.

3. If time allows, cover and refrigerate for 1–2 hours or until needed.

4. Heat some oil in a frying pan and add some of the meatballs, pressing them down gently to flatten them slightly (don't crowd the pan, better to cook them in batches). Cook for about 5 minutes, turning them over at least once, until cooked through and crusty brown on the outside. Drain on kitchen paper and keep warm.

5. Repeat with the remaining mixture until all the meatballs are cooked.

Slow-Cooked Beef in Red Wine

Visit any region of France and you are likely to come across a version of Boeuf en Daube or Daube de Boeuf – beef slowly cooked in red wine with vegetables and seasonings which always include a little orange peel. Its name comes from daubière, the special casserole in which it was traditionally made. The dish needs to be started at least the day before you serve it because the beef needs to marinate in red wine for about 24 hours before cooking. Even better is to marinate it one day, cook it the next, then leave it to cool and reheat it on day three – by which time the flavours will have developed to a wonderful richness. Serve it with Panisses (Chickpea Fritters on page 59), mashed potatoes, rice or pasta such as tagliatelle.

Serves 6

1.25kg/3 lb lean stewing steak, cut into pieces about 5cm/2 in
2 large onions, roughly chopped
2 carrots, thickly sliced
2 celery sticks, thickly sliced
2 garlic cloves, finely chopped
2 bay leaves
2–3 sprigs of thyme
Sprig of rosemary
Large strip of orange peel (with no white pith attached)
Freshly milled black pepper
300ml/½ pt red wine
3 tbsp olive oil
125g/5 oz lean streaky bacon (unsmoked) or pancetta, cut into thin strips or small cubes
400g can chopped tomatoes
150ml/¼ pt beef stock
About 24 olives (optional)

1. Put the beef into a large non-metal bowl and add the onions, carrots, celery, garlic, herbs, orange peel and a good grinding of black pepper. Pour the wine over and mix well. Cover and leave to marinate (in the refrigerator) for about 24 hours.

2. Heat a large frying pan, add the olive oil and bacon and cook, stirring occasionally, until golden brown. With a slotted spoon, transfer the bacon into a large ovenproof casserole.

3. Lift the beef out of the marinade and dab it on kitchen paper. Quickly brown the meat in the hot frying pan in small batches and transfer to the casserole.

4. With the slotted spoon lift the vegetables out of the marinade and add them to the frying pan. Cook quickly for about 5 minutes, stirring occasionally, until just beginning to brown. Add them to the casserole.

5. Tip the marinade into the frying pan and add the tomatoes and stock. Bring just to the boil and pour the mixture over the contents of the casserole. Tuck the herbs and orange peel down into the juices.

6. Cover and put the casserole into the oven at 150°C, fan 130°C, 300°F, gas 2. Cook for about 2½ hours or until the beef is tender.

7. Stir in the olives if using.

Beef Stifado

This rich Greek stew, with equal quantities of meat and onions, can also be made with pork, chicken or rabbit. It tastes even better when reheated.

Serves 4

4 tbsp olive oil
1kg/2¼ lb lean stewing or braising steak, cut into large cubes
1kg/2¼ lb onions, roughly chopped
2 garlic cloves, finely chopped
5 tbsp red wine vinegar
300ml/½ pt red wine
400g can whole tomatoes
2 bay leaves
1 tsp ground cumin
½ tsp ground allspice
6 whole cloves
1 cinnamon stick
Freshly milled salt and black pepper

1. Preheat the oven to 170°C, fan 150°C, 325°F, gas 3.

2. Heat a large, heavy-based ovenproof casserole on the hob. Add half the oil and brown the beef in small batches, lifting it out on to a plate with a slotted spoon.

3. Add the remaining oil to the pan, add the onions and cook oven medium heat for about 10 minutes, stirring occasionally, until beginning to soften and turn golden brown.

4. Add the garlic and vinegar and let it bubble until it has reduced to almost nothing.

5. Add the beef and its juices then stir in the wine, tomatoes (roughly chopping them as you add them), herbs and spices. Season with salt and pepper.

6. Bring just to the boil and cover tightly.

7. Put into the hot oven and cook for about 2 hours until the beef is very tender.

Grilled Pasta with Vegetables and Beef

This is based on a dish enjoyed recently during a short trip to northern Italy. Vary the meat and vegetables according to your taste. Try adding a little chopped fresh chilli or some chopped capers too. Serve with a crunchy green salad dressed with oil and vinegar.

Serves 4

4 tbsp olive oil
4 shallots, finely chopped
1 aubergine, cut into small dice
2 garlic cloves, finely chopped
25g/9 oz lean minced beef, pork or chicken
150g/5½ oz mushrooms, thinly sliced
1 red or yellow pepper, seeds removed and finely chopped
1 tbsp dried oregano
Freshly milled salt and pepper
500g carton or jar of passata (sieved tomatoes)
About 300g/10½ oz large pasta tubes, such as pennoni
4 generous tbsp freshly grated Parmesan cheese

1. Heat the oil in a large pan, add the shallots and aubergine and cook over medium heat for about 10 minutes until soft and light golden brown.

2. Add the garlic and the mince (broken into chunks) and cook for a few minutes, stirring occasionally, until the beef begins to brown.

3. Add the mushrooms, pepper, oregano and seasoning, then stir in the passata. Bring just to the boil, cover and simmer gently for about 30 minutes, stirring occasionally.

4. Meanwhile, cook the pasta following the packet instructions.

5. Drain the pasta and stir it into the hot sauce. Tip the mixture into an oiled flameproof dish and scatter the cheese over the top.

6. Put under a hot grill until golden brown, crisp and bubbling.

Chicken with Olives and Preserved Lemon

This is based on one of the best-known Moroccan tagines or stews. Traditionally, it would be cooked slowly in a conical earthenware pot (also called a tagine). Preserved lemons are usually stripped of their flesh and only the peel is used but I prefer simply to remove the pips and cut the rest (peel and fruit) into thin slices. Serve with couscous and a green vegetable or salad.

Serves 4–6

2 tbsp olive oil
2 medium onions, finely chopped
2 garlic cloves, finely chopped
Pinch of saffron strands
1 tsp ground ginger
½ tsp ground cumin
500ml/18 fl oz chicken stock
1 large chicken, weighing about 2kg/4½ lb, trimmed of excess fat around the cavity openings
2 pickled lemons (see above), thinly sliced
115g/4 oz mixed olives
Freshly milled black pepper
About 2 tbsp chopped fresh coriander
About 1 tbsp chopped fresh parsley (preferably the flat-leaf variety)

1. Heat the oil in a large, heavy-based pan that is large enough to take the whole chicken. Add the onions and cook over medium heat for about 10 minutes, stirring occasionally, until softened but not browned. Add the garlic, saffron, ginger and cumin and cook for a few minutes more, stirring frequently.

2. Add the stock to the onion mixture and bring to a gentle simmer. Add the chicken, turning it so that it is coated with the sauce.

3. Cover and simmer very gently for about 1½ hours, turning the chicken occasionally, until it is tender and cooked through.

4. Add the pickled lemon slices and olives, and season with black pepper. Cover and simmer gently for a further 15 minutes.

5. Lift the chicken out of the sauce, cover and keep warm.

6. Allow the sauce to stand for 5–10 minutes then skim any excess fat from the top. Bring the sauce to the boil and bubble briskly until it has reduced slightly. Stir in the coriander and parsley.

7. Spoon the sauce, lemon and olives over and around the chicken and serve.

To cook in the oven:
1. Follow steps 1 and 2 above, while preheating the oven to 180°C, fan 160°F, 350°F, gas 4.

2. Cover the pan, put into the hot oven and cook for about 1½ hours, spooning the liquid over the chicken occasionally.

3. Add the pickled lemon slices and olives, and season with black pepper. Either cover and continue cooking for a further 15 minutes, or remove the cover to allow the chicken to brown a little on top.

4. Follow steps 5–7 above.

Chicken Cacciatore

Cacciatore is Italian for 'hunter' so this dish is often called Hunter Style or Hunters' Chicken. It usually contains onions, tomatoes and herbs. When wine is added it's usually white, though I'm quite happy to use red.

Serves 6

2 tbsp olive oil
140g/5 oz pancetta cubes or diced unsmoked bacon
12 baby onions or shallots
6 chicken thighs, trimmed of excess skin and fat
6 chicken drumsticks
2 garlic cloves, finely chopped
400g can chopped tomatoes
300ml/½ pt red wine
Freshly milled salt and black pepper
175g/6 oz button mushrooms

1. Put 1 tbsp oil into a large, heavy-based pan and add the pancetta or bacon. Cook over medium heat, stirring occasionally, until lightly browned.

2. Add the onions to the pan and cook, stirring occasionally, until golden brown. With a slotted spoon, transfer the pancetta and onions to a plate.

3. Add the chicken pieces to the pan and brown quickly on all sides.

4. Return the onion mixture to the pan and add the garlic, tomatoes, wine and seasoning.

5. Bring just to the boil, cover so that the lid is just slightly askew, and simmer gently for about 40 minutes.

6. About 10 minutes before serving, heat the remaining oil in a pan, add the mushrooms and cook quickly until golden brown.

7. Stir the mushrooms into the chicken and serve.

Chicken Pilaf with Saffron Yogurt

Pilaf is a traditional dish in Turkey, made with vegetables, fish, chicken, meat, game or a mixture of nuts and dried fruit. It is just as delicious made with bulgur wheat in place of rice.

Serves 4

Large pinch of saffron strands
200ml carton Greek yogurt
3 tbsp olive oil
50g/1¾ oz flaked almonds
8 chicken thighs
1 medium onion, thinly sliced
100g/3½ oz button mushrooms, sliced
225g/8 oz long grain rice
600ml/1 pt chicken stock

1. To make the saffron yogurt, crush the saffron strands (with the back of a spoon or with a pestle and mortar), add 1 tbsp boiling water and leave to stand for 10 minutes. Stir the saffron and its liquid into the yogurt, cover and chill until required.

2. Heat a large non-stick frying pan and add 2 tbsp oil. Add the almonds and cook, stirring, until golden brown. Lift out and drain on kitchen paper.

3. Add the remaining 1 tbsp oil to the pan, add the chicken and brown quickly all over. Lift out and drain on kitchen paper.

4. Add the onion and mushrooms to the pan and cook, stirring occasionally, until the onions are soft and beginning to brown.

5. Stir the rice into the onion mixture and cook, stirring, for about 2 minutes.

6. Stir in the stock and add the chicken, pushing it gently under the liquid.

7. Cover and cook gently for 15–20 minutes, stirring once or twice, until the chicken is cooked, the rice is tender and the stock has been absorbed.

8. Scatter the almonds over the pilaf and serve immediately with the saffron yogurt.

Turkey in a Parmesan Crust

A version of this delicious dish is served in much of Italy. It's equally good made with pork steaks or with flattened chicken breasts and served with buttered tagliatelle and a green vegetable or salad. My family particularly like it with a serving of Tomato Sauce (see page 66).

Serves 4

4 tbsp flour
Freshly milled salt and black pepper
1 large egg
About 6 tbsp freshly grated Parmesan cheese
4 turkey breast steaks
Olive oil

1. Put the flour into a shallow dish and season it well with salt and pepper. Break the egg into a second dish and beat until smooth. Put the Parmesan into another dish.

2. Coat each turkey breast first in flour, shaking off the excess. Now dip it in the beaten egg and, finally, in the cheese. Repeat with the remaining turkey.

3. Heat a large frying pan and add some oil. Cook the turkey for a few minutes on each side or until golden brown and cooked through.

4. Serve immediately.

5

DESSERTS & PASTRIES

Dine in almost any region of the Mediterranean and your meal will invariably end with fruit – a showcase to whatever is ripe and in season. At its simplest you may be offered a bowl of whole fruits (grapes, figs, apricots, plums) or a platter of fruit that has been carefully prepared, sliced and ready to eat (melon, mango, peach, persimmon) or perhaps a selection of fresh and dried fruits (apricots, dates, figs). And it is remarkable how something as ordinary as a bowl of oranges is transformed into something sublime simply by removing the rind and pith and slicing into thin circles before sprinkling with slivered pistachio nuts, orange flower water or a dusting of cinnamon.

While fruit plays a leading role in Mediterranean cuisines, desserts and pastries are likely to be kept for high days and holidays, with many of the traditional recipes being bought from specialist producers and shops rather than being home-made. Instead of being served at mealtimes, sweet concoctions are more likely to be offered in small portions to accompany a cup of strong coffee in the middle of the morning or afternoon. In comparison, the British tradition of serving pudding at the end of a meal continues, and it is with this in mind that the recipes in this final chapter have been selected. Each one is simple, easy to make and guaranteed to deliver a substantial helping of 'wow' factor!

Lemon Tart

Lemon is a great fruit, usually imported from Spain or Cyprus, and lemon tart must be one of the best desserts ever invented. Serve it dusted with icing sugar. A fruit sauce, such as raspberry, goes well with it too.

Serves 8–10

Pastry:
175g/6 oz plain flour
Pinch of salt
115g/4 oz butter, cut into cubes
2 tbsp caster sugar
1 egg yolk

Filling:
5 large eggs
225g/8 oz caster sugar
150ml carton double cream
3 or 4 unwaxed lemons

1.   Sift the flour and salt into a large bowl and rub in the butter until the mixture resembles fine breadcrumbs. Stir in the sugar. Make a well in the centre of the mixture and add the egg yolk and 1 tbsp cold water. Mix well, working the mixture into a smooth dough, adding a few extra drops of water if necessary. (Alternatively, buzz the flour, salt, sugar and butter in a food processor, add the egg yolk and water and process until a dough forms.) Cover and chill for 20 minutes.

2.   Put a flat baking sheet into the oven and preheat to 190°C, fan 170°C, 375°F, gas 5.

3.   Meanwhile, make the filling. Put the eggs, sugar and cream into a large bowl. Finely grate the zest from three lemons and add to the mixture. Squeeze the juice from the lemons to make 150ml/¼ pt and add this to the bowl. Use a wooden spoon to stir the mixture until it is well blended.

4.   On a lightly floured surface, roll out the pastry and use it to line a flan tin measuring 25cm/10 in diameter and 2.5cm/1 in deep. Prick the base lightly with a fork and chill for 10 minutes.

5. Line the pastry case with a circle of non-stick or grease-proof paper and half-fill with baking beans, dried beans or rice. Put into the hot oven and cook for 15 minutes. Carefully remove the beans and paper and continue cooking for a further 10 minutes.

6. Pour the filling into the cooked pastry case, reduce the heat to 150°C, fan 130°C, 300°F, gas 2, and cook for about 30 minutes or until the filling is only just set (don't worry if it still wobbles just a little).

7. Leave to cool for about 1 hour before serving at room temperature or chilled.

Peach and Almond Tart

A tart that is equally delicious made with nectarines, apricots or pears, either fresh ripe ones or drained canned. Take care when adding the almond extract – its flavour can be quite powerful. Serve the tart with crème fraîche or thick Greek yogurt.

Serves 8–10

Pastry:
175g/6 oz plain flour
Pinch of salt
115g/4 oz butter, cut into cubes
2 tbsp caster sugar
1 egg yolk

3 or 4 firm ripe peaches

Filling:
150g/5½ oz softened butter
150g/5½ oz caster sugar
Few drops almond extract
4 medium eggs, lightly beaten
3 tbsp plain flour
150g/5½ oz ground almonds
3 tbsp milk

Glaze:
3 tbsp apricot jam

1. Make the pastry. Sift the flour and salt into a large bowl and rub in the butter until the mixture resembles fine breadcrumbs. Stir in the sugar. Make a well in the centre of the mixture and add the egg yolk and 1 tbsp cold water. Mix well, working the mixture into a smooth dough, adding a few extra drops of water if necessary. (Alternatively, buzz the flour, salt, sugar and butter in a food processor, add the egg yolk and water and process until a dough forms.) Cover and chill for 20 minutes.

2. Put a flat baking sheet into the oven and preheat to 190°C, fan 170°C, 375°F, gas 5.

3. On a lightly floured surface, roll out the pastry and use it to line a flan tin measuring 25cm/10 in diameter and 2.5cm/1 in deep. Prick the base lightly with a fork and chill for 10 minutes.

4.   Line the pastry case with a circle of non-stick or grease-proof paper and half-fill with baking beans, dried beans or rice. Put into the hot oven and cook for 15 minutes. Carefully remove the beans and paper and continue cooking for a further 10 minutes. Remove from the oven and leave to cool.

5.   Put the peaches into a large bowl and cover with boiling water. Leave to stand for a minute or two after which the skins should peel off easily. Cut each peach into quarters, removing the stones.

6.   Make the filling. Beat the butter, sugar and almond extract until light and creamy. Gradually beat in the eggs then stir in the flour, almonds and milk.

7.   Spread the filling in the cooled pastry case. Arrange the peach quarters on top, like the spokes of a wheel, pressing them lightly into the filling.

8.   Reduce the oven temperature to 170°C, fan 150°C, 325°F, gas 3. Put the tart in the hot oven and cook for about 45 minutes or until the centre is just firm to the touch and the top is deep golden brown. Leave to cool.

9.   When the tart is cool, carefully remove it from the tin.

10. Make the glaze by heating the jam with 1 tbsp water. For a smooth result (which is optional) push through a sieve. Carefully brush the glaze over the top of the tart.

French Apple Tart

The true home of the classic Tarte aux Pommes is the apple-growing region of Normandy, far north of the Mediterranean. However, since generic apple tarts seem to be sold all over France (and it does happen to be one of my family's favourite desserts) I make no apologies for including it here.

Serves 8–10

Pastry:
175g/6 oz plain flour
Pinch of salt
115g/4 oz butter, cut into cubes
2 tbsp caster sugar
1 egg yolk

Filling:
9 crisp eating apples
Juice of 1 lemon
15g/½ oz butter
55g/2 oz caster sugar

Glaze:
3 tbsp apricot jam

1. Make the pastry. Sift the flour and salt into a large bowl and rub in the butter until the mixture resembles fine breadcrumbs. Stir in the sugar. Make a well in the centre of the mixture and add the egg yolk and 1 tbsp cold water. Mix well, working the mixture into a smooth dough, adding a few extra drops of water if necessary. (Alternatively, buzz the flour, salt, sugar and butter in a food processor, add the egg yolk and water and process until a dough forms.) Cover and chill for 20 minutes.

2. Put a flat baking sheet into the oven and preheat to 190°C, fan 170°C, 375°F, gas 5.

3. On a lightly floured surface, roll out the pastry and use it to line a flan tin measuring 25cm/10 in diameter and 2.5cm/1 in deep. Prick the base lightly with a fork and chill for 10 minutes.

4. Meanwhile, peel, core and slice 6 apples and put them in a pan with 2 tbsp water and about two-thirds of the lemon juice. Bring to the boil, cover and simmer gently for 15–20 minutes, stirring occasionally, until the apples are very soft. Mash to a rough purée and stir in the butter and half the sugar.

5. Peel, core and thinly slice the remaining apples, tossing them in the remaining lemon juice and sugar.

6. Spread the puréed apple in the tart case and arrange the slices, overlapping in concentric circles, on top.

7. Lower the oven temperature to 180°C, fan 160°C, 350°F, gas 4. Put the tart into the hot oven and cook for about 30 minutes until the apples are golden brown on their edges. Leave to cool.

8. When the tart is cool, remove from the tin.

9. To make the glaze, heat the jam with 1 tbsp water. For a smooth result (which is optional) push through a sieve. Gently brush the glaze over the top of the tart.

Panna Cotta

Panna cotta is Italian for 'cooked cream'. It always impresses, yet it's so simple to make and can even be prepared one or two days before you intend to serve it. Depending on the season, accompany it with some fresh soft fruit or some dried fruits simmered in red wine with spices.

Serves 6

4 gelatine leaves
500ml/18 fl oz milk
500ml/18 fl oz double cream
175g/6 oz caster sugar
2 vanilla pods or 3 tsp vanilla extract

1. Soak the gelatine leaves in cold water for about 5 minutes until soft.

2. Meanwhile, put the milk and cream into a large saucepan and add the sugar. If using vanilla pods, split them lengthways and scrape the seeds out into the milk mixture (alternatively, add the vanilla extract). Bring just to the boil and remove from the heat. (Alternatively, you could bring to the boil in the microwave.)

3. Lift the gelatine out of the water, squeezing it lightly, and add to the hot vanilla cream, stirring well until dissolved.

4. Strain the mixture (through a sieve) into individual moulds or one large one.

5. Leave to cool then refrigerate for at least 2 hours or until set.

6. To serve, run a knife around the edge of the mould, dip its base in hot water for a few seconds then turn out on to a serving plate.

Pears in Rose Water

*The syrup in which the poached pears are served is mildly
perfumed with rose water (see page 17). Adding a couple of split
cardamom seeds in step 1 adds another flavour dimension. For a
rose-pink syrup, simply use white instead of golden caster sugar
and colour the syrup with a little food colouring. Serve with crisp
biscuits such as amaretti and/or thick Greek yogurt.*

Serves 6

150g/5 oz golden caster sugar
6 firm ripe pears
½ lemon
Rose water

1. Put the sugar into a saucepan (just large enough to hold
   the pears in a single layer) with 300ml/½ pt water. Heat
   until dissolved.

2. Peel the pears, leaving them whole. Rub the flesh with the
   cut side of the lemon – this prevents them from browning.

3. Put the pears into the sugar syrup and add sufficient water
   to just cover them.

4. Bring to the boil, cover and simmer for 20–30 minutes or
   until just tender.

5. Gently lift the pears into a serving dish.

6. Bubble the syrup rapidly to reduce and thicken it. Remove
   from the heat and leave to cool a little before adding rose
   water to taste. Pour over the pears and leave to cool
   completely. Chill until required.

Pistachio Ice Slice

Pistachio nuts lend their delicate flavour to many a Mediterranean dessert. This luxurious ice cream is one of my favourites. Serve it in slices sprinkled with a few extra chopped pistachios.

Serves about 6

125g/4½ oz shelled pistachio nuts
5 tbsp caster sugar
284ml carton double cream, chilled
425g carton custard, chilled

1. Put the pistachios into a food processor, add the sugar and buzz until finely ground.

2. Tip the cream into a jug and add the custard and pistachio mixture. With a whisk, stir well.

3. Cover and refrigerate for about 30 minutes by which time the sugar should have dissolved.

4. Churn the mixture in an ice cream machine. Alternatively, pour the mixture into a plastic freezer box, cover and freeze, taking it out every 30–45 minutes to stir it. Each time you stir the mixture, scrape the ice crystals that have formed around the edges, push them to the centre of the container and mash them (it's a good idea to set a timer as a reminder). When the ice is thick and creamy, it's ready.

5. Spoon the ice cream into a rectangular loaf tin and freeze until firm.

6. To serve, turn the loaf out on to a serving plate by dipping the basin briefly (about 30 seconds) into hot water to loosen it first. If the ice cream is really hard, leave it in the refrigerator for about 20 minutes to soften slightly before serving.

7. Cut into slices using a warm sharp knife.

Fig and Mascarpone Ice

This ice cream has distinct Italian overtones. It's quite rich so serve small scoops with lightly poached fruit such as apricots or with warm Almond Cake with Lemon and Honey (page 122).

Serves 6–8

150g/5 oz ready-to-eat dried figs
250g carton mascarpone cheese
200g carton Greek yogurt
2 tbsp caster sugar
2 tbsp orange liqueur

1. Put the figs into a food processor or blender. Add the mascarpone cheese, yogurt, sugar and liqueur. Blend until smooth, scraping down the sides if necessary.

2. Cover and refrigerate for about 30 minutes until chilled.

3. Churn the mixture in an ice cream machine then transfer to a suitable container and freeze until required. Alternatively, pour the mixture into a plastic freezer box, cover and freeze, taking it out every 30–45 minutes to stir it. Each time you stir the mixture, scrape the ice crystals that have formed around the edges, push them to the centre of the container and mash them (it's a good idea to set a timer as a reminder). When the ice is thick and creamy, it's ready to serve.

Baklava

Baklava is one of a range of sweet pastries served in Greece and Turkey. This version is made with pistachios but it is equally delicious made with walnuts or almonds and flavoured with a little ground cinnamon and nutmeg. Serve the pastries slightly warm or at room temperature, with or without a spoonful of thick Greek yogurt.

Makes about 12

300g/11 oz shelled pistachio nuts
85g/3 oz light muscovado sugar
12 sheets of filo pastry
About 175g/6 oz unsalted butter, melted

Syrup:
175g/6 oz sugar
2 generous tbsp honey (a Greek honey with a good flavour is preferable)
1 tbsp lemon juice
2 tbsp rose water (see page 17)

1. Put the nuts into a food processor with the sugar and buzz until very finely chopped.

2. Preheat the oven to 180°C, fan 160°C, 350°F, gas 4.

3. Choose a shallow baking tin that is just slightly smaller than the pastry sheets and brush it with melted butter. Lay four sheets of pastry in the tin, brushing each one lightly with butter.

4. Spread one-third of the nut mixture over the pastry and top with two pastry sheets (brushing each one with butter). Repeat, using another third of the nut mixture and two pastry sheets, buttered. Top with the remaining nuts and follow with the final four pastry sheets, buttering each one. Tuck the pastry edges down the inside of the tin and brush the top liberally with butter.

5. With a sharp knife, cut the pastry right through to the bottom, making parallel strips and cutting the strips diagonally into diamond shapes.

6. Put into the hot oven and cook for 30–40 minutes until crisp and golden brown.

7. Meanwhile, make the syrup by heating the sugar, honey and lemon juice with 100ml/3½ fl oz water until dissolved (use the hob or the microwave). Bubble gently for about 5 minutes, then stir in the rose water and leave the mixture to cool while the pastries cook.

8. Pour the syrup over the hot pastries (still in their tin) and leave to cool completely before cutting and lifting out for serving.

Zabaglione

Here is one of the best-known Italian desserts. The egg yolks thicken to develop a light, foamy concoction. Serve it warm in pretty stemmed glasses with crisp biscuits such as amaretti. Alternatively, spoon it like a sauce over fruit, ice cream, cakes or pastries.

Serves 4

4 medium egg yolks
4 tbsp caster sugar
8 tbsp Marsala (see page 14)

1. Put all the ingredients in a double boiler or in a bowl standing in a large pan of hot (not boiling) water.

2. Over a low heat and using a balloon whisk, lightly beat the mixture until it thickens to a texture that is thick, pale and foamy, and starts to come away from the sides of the bowl (this could take 15 minutes or so).

3. Serve immediately.

Turkish Delightful Ice

This perfumed ice reminds me of the Middle Eastern jellied sweetmeat Turkish Delight. Serve it topped with a sprinkling of chopped pistachio nuts, toasted slivers of almonds, hazelnuts or pine nuts, or chocolate shavings.

Serves 4–6

200g carton Greek yogurt, chilled
142ml carton double cream, chilled
85g/3 oz caster sugar
Juice of 1 small lemon
4 tbsp orange liqueur
Orange flower water
Rose water (see page 17)

1. Tip the yogurt and cream into a large jug. With a whisk, stir in the sugar, lemon juice and liqueur. Add orange flower water and rose water, in equal quantities and a small amount at a time, to taste.

2. Cover and refrigerate for 20–30 minutes or until well chilled.

3. Churn the mixture in an ice cream machine then transfer to a suitable container and freeze until required. Alternatively, pour the mixture into a plastic freezer box, cover and freeze, taking it out every 30–45 minutes to stir it. Each time you stir the mixture, scrape the ice crystals that have formed around the edges, push them to the centre of the container and mash them (it's a good idea to set a timer as a reminder). When the ice is thick and creamy, it's ready to serve.

Rice Pudding with Rose Water and Vanilla

A sweet and creamy dessert with a delicate flavour. Serve it warm (though I particularly like it chilled) with a drizzle of runny honey and a scattering of chopped pistachio nuts.

Serves 4–6

75g/2¾ oz pudding rice (or use a risotto rice such as arborio)
25g/1 oz caster sugar
2 tbsp runny honey
850ml/1½ pt milk (full or semi-skimmed)
142ml carton double cream
2 tbsp rose water, or to taste (see page 17)
¼ tsp vanilla extract

1. Put the rice into a saucepan with the sugar and honey. Stir in the milk and cream.

2. Bring to the boil and simmer gently for about 45 minutes until the rice is soft and the pudding is thick and creamy. Stir occasionally at first and then frequently towards the end of cooking (to prevent the mixture sticking to the bottom of the pan).

3. Stir in rose water to taste and vanilla, then leave to stand until required.

Almond Cake with Lemon and Honey

Serve this soft cake warm as a dessert with Greek yogurt. Alternatively, leave it to cool completely, cut into wedges and accompany it with a cup of good strong coffee.

Serves 6–8

Cake:
115g/4 oz softened unsalted butter, plus extra for greasing
85g/3 oz caster sugar
115g/4 oz semolina
85g/3 oz ground almonds
2 medium eggs
Finely grated rind of 1 lemon
4 tbsp lemon juice

Topping:
4 tbsp lemon juice
4 tbsp runny honey
1 tbsp sesame seeds, lightly toasted

1. Lightly butter a 20 cm/8 in cake tin and line its base with baking paper. Preheat the oven to 180°C, fan 160°C, 350°F, gas 4.

2. Put the butter into a mixing bowl, add the remaining cake ingredients and beat well to make a smooth batter.

3. Spoon the mixture into the prepared tin and level the surface.

4. Put into the hot oven and cook for 20–30 minutes until the top is golden brown and the cake is cooked through (it should feel just firm to the touch and a skewer inserted in the centre should come out clean).

5. Leave to stand for 5 minutes before turning the cake out on to a wire rack.

6. For the topping, stir together the lemon juice and honey (you may need to heat it) and spoon it slowly over the cake until it has all been absorbed.

7. Sprinkle the sesame seeds over the top and leave to cool completely.

Baked Ricotta Puddings with Figs and Honey

These puddings can be cooked in advance and reheated gently in the microwave just before serving. I like to serve the figs at room temperature but you could drizzle them with a little honey and pop them under a hot grill until soft and bubbling.

Serves 4

500g/1 lb 2 oz ricotta cheese
50g/1¾ oz soft brown sugar
2 medium eggs, lightly beaten
Seeds of 2 vanilla pods
About 6 fresh ripe figs, halved or quartered
Runny honey
Toasted pine nuts, to garnish

1. Preheat the oven to 180°C, fan 160°C, 350°F, gas 4.

2. Put the cheese into a large bowl with the sugar, eggs and vanilla seeds and beat until smooth.

3. Spoon the mixture into four lightly greased ovenproof dishes or moulds.

4. Put into the hot oven and cook for 35–40 minutes until risen and golden brown on top.

5. Turn out the puddings and serve warm with the figs, all drizzled with honey to taste and garnished with pine nuts.

INDEX